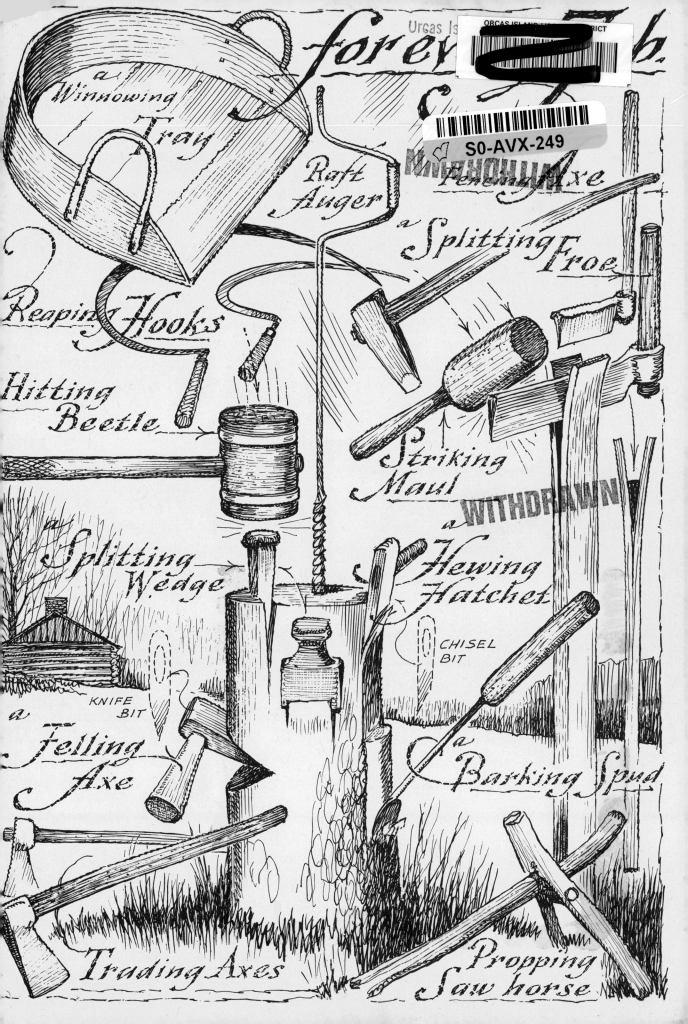

A Museum
of
Early
American
Tools

a MUSEUM
of
Early American
TOOLS

by

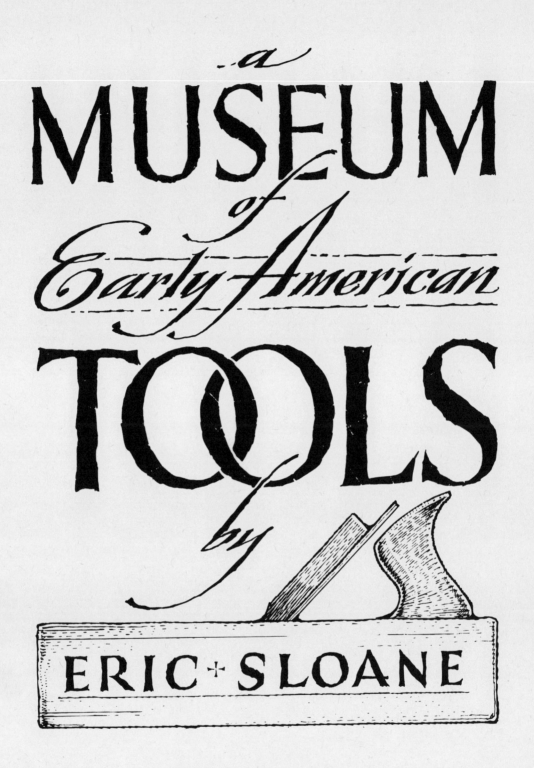

ERIC + SLOANE

FUNK & WAGNALLS
NEW YORK

Copyright © 1964 by Wilfred Funk, Inc.

Library of Congress Catalogue Card Number: 64-13741

Printed in the United States of America

Published in Canada by

Fitzhenry & Whiteside Limited, Toronto

ISBN 0-308-70046-5

13   14   15   16   17   18   19   20

*This sketchbook is dedicated to the
unrecorded pioneer Americans who
fashioned their own tools. Although
mass production has made their old
tools obsolete, along with Early American
individualism, these ancient implements
are symbols of a sincerity, an integrity,
and an excellency that the
unionized craftsman of today might do
well to emulate.*

The Carpenter who builds a good House to defend us from Wind and Weather, is far more serviceable than the curious Carver who employs his art to please his Fancy...

...from an old tool pamphlet...
...1719

Author's Note

I like the sound of the word museum. Perhaps because the word root refers less to an actual collection of things than to the musing, cogitating, and reflecting that one does while beholding a collection.

Nowadays we use the word museum to identify a big, housed collection, but in the days of Early America it usually meant a simple library or some printed collection of facts. There were magazinelike books, such as "Merry's *Museum*," and there were newspaperlike publications, such as "The Farmer's *Museum*," but the fine word museum has since drifted from the world of writing. Because it is my hobby to recapture what I believe to be the good things of the past, I hope the reader will accept and enjoy my title, *A Museum of Early American Tools*.

The word magazine was first used to identify what we now might call a museum; it then meant "storehouse," or "housed collection" (powder magazine, for instance). And the first printed magazines were (like the newspapers of that day) printed on one piece of paper and folded once or perhaps twice—never in the book-form of today's magazine.

In presenting my collection of drawings as a museum, I hope that it will, like a scrapbook, induce musing and reflecting, and that it will draw the reader back into the quite different world of Early America. The rambling sequence of subjects is no accident: I would like my reader to "stroll" through this book as he would through a museum.

We might regard some of the old tools as clumsy or ugly unless we look at them in terms of the century in which they were used. Many of today's tools would have been considered ugly, clumsy, and completely undesirable by the early craftsmen. The steel and plastic handles we now have, for example, lack the spring and "feel" of seasoned wood that experts know. Shovels were made of wood not because of a lack of metal (as many assume) but because it was supposed that grain and apples were harmed by contact with metal. You might think of a wooden shovel as being short-lived, yet, although thousands of wooden shovels are to be found in antique shops and collections, almost no early metal shovels remain.

Most of today's tools have the cheapness of mass production; the old hand-made tools often had design that made them examples of fine art. Lumber cut and sold as a "two by four" was once an honest two inches by four inches; even today there are people who are shocked to learn that our lumber, because it is measured before being trimmed and planed, is sold at a quite untrue measurement. Builders who constructed rooms that were not accurately square (and why should they be?) are now regarded as slipshod and careless; yet the old buildings have stood the test much better than will many we are now building, for the joints and braces were made with much greater care than today's craftsmen consider "necessary." Floor boards were never the same width at one end as they were at the other. Quaint or poor workmanship? Not at all. The finished effect is finer than the monotony of today's narrow-width floor boards. A building pinned together with hand-whittled wooden pins? We don't have to do that sort of thing today! But if we built for lastingness and for handing down to future generations we would do so, for wooden pins work much better than nails: they hold tighter, they don't rust and rot the beams.

While I was putting this book together, my neighbor bought a good new saw and left it out overnight in the dew. Its shiny newness had given way to the orange of rust, and he telephoned me to ask for help in removing it. I took it to clean and loaned him one of my early saws to use in the meantime. The old saw was one I found in the stone wall of an ancient barn. It is still sharp and clean of rust.

And so it goes. The craftsman of yesterday might look like a poorly informed man only before we take a longer and a better look. His tools might appear pathetically poor, but his ways were honest and lasting and beautiful to an extent that is today deemed over and above requirements. How poor and dishonest and ugly and temporary are the results of so many modern workers whose constant aim is more to make the most money from their profession instead of producing the most honest and beautiful and lasting things. I feel that a good way of studying the conscience and personality of the anonymous pioneer American—so that I may emulate some of his ways—is by collecting and analyzing the tools with which he worked.

As a collector of early tools, I have also been a collector of information. Antique implements have a price tag on them, but for the information that has been priceless and gratis, I am indebted to the men at Doylestown, Shelburne, Winterthur, Cooperstown, Sturbridge, Williamsburg, and Saugus. I learned much from two excellent books, Mercer's *Ancient Carpenters' Tools and* Wildung's *Woodworking* Tools, *and from the Early American Industries Association's publication,* The Chronicle.

Eric Sloane

Weather Hill

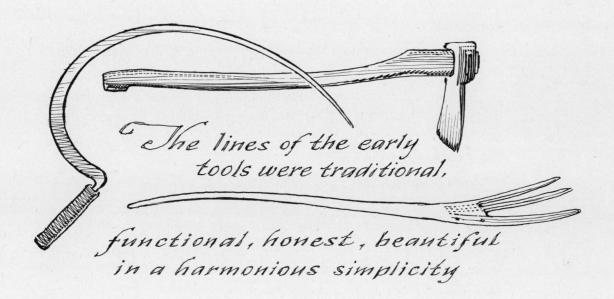

"The lines of the early
tools were traditional,
functional, honest, beautiful
in a harmonious simplicity

Contents

a Museum
of
Early
American
Tools

The Romance of Tools.

Finding an ancient tool in a stone fence or in a dark corner of some decaying barn is receiving a symbol from another world, for it gives you a particular and interesting contact with the past. Men used to build and create as much for future generations as for their own needs, so their tools have a special message for us and our time. When you hold an early implement, when you close your hand over the worn wooden handle, you know exactly how it felt to the craftsman whose hand had smoothed it to its rich patina. In that instant you are as close to that craftsman as you can be—even closer than if you live in the house that he built or sit in the chair that he made. In that moment you are near to another being in another life, and you are that much richer.

Why an ancient tool should be closer to the early craftsman than a modern tool is to a modern workman is not readily understood by most people. Even the ardent collector is sometimes unaware of the reason an ancient tool meant so much to its user. But reason there is. Henry Ward Beecher said it nicely when he explained that "a tool is but the extension of a man's hand." Whereas today's implements are designed with the idea of "getting a job done quickly," there was an added quality to the early implements and an added quality to early workmanship too. For, like the nails on a beast's paws, the old tools were so much an extension of a man's hand or an added appendage to his arm, that the resulting workmanship seemed to flow directly from the body of the maker and to carry something of himself into the work. True, by looking at an old house or an old piece of furniture, you can imagine the maker much more clearly than you can by beholding anything made today.

The early implement was also a piece of art, as much as the work it

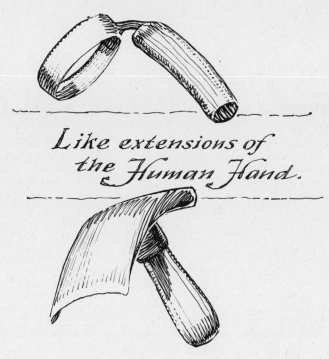

Like extensions of the Human Hand.

fashioned, for the worker designed his tools too. In Early America the ironworkers forged only the cutting blade; they gave no thought to the design of the wooden handle and the rest of the finished tool. Plane blades and even knife-blades were hand-forged and sold like axe heads, and the craftsman was left to make his own wooden "hand" to hold the "fingernail," or cutting part. A small hand needed a small handle and a big hand needed a big handle; the man who used an apprentice had notches in his big plane that enabled the apprentice to help push it along with a stick.

A man whose architectural creations followed the Greek or Roman tradition would find it natural to include Greek or Roman artistic touches in the ornamentation of his implements. Decoration on the early tool, however, sprang from the pride of the maker rather than from any custom.

The feeling that certain tools had souls of their own was not unusual; an axe might be marked "Tom" or "Jack" simply because the owner felt it was a companion worthy of a pet name. All this sounds strangely superstitious. Yet today motor trucks are often named "Sally" or "Babe"; boats almost always have names; even large machine tools, such as presses or bulldozers, are graced with pet names.

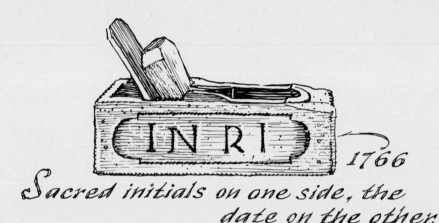

Sacred initials on one side, the date on the other.

The religious man probably felt that sacred initials or Biblical quotations might have their effect upon the work done by that tool. Perhaps mindful that the carpenter Jesus once worked with such tools, some of the early woodworking implements have crosses carved upon them.

One of the finer pieces in a recent showing of modern art was a piece of steel that curved like a bird's wing. It was set into a square block of wood and its title in the catalogue was "Number 1760." The artist had an even more honest sense of beauty than a sense of humor, for if you looked closely and with an informed eye, you could recognize the piece as the head of an Early American "goose wing" broad axe. In the back of the blade, the year 1760 had been marked, which, of course, explained the title. To many it was, at first, the most beautiful piece of art there,

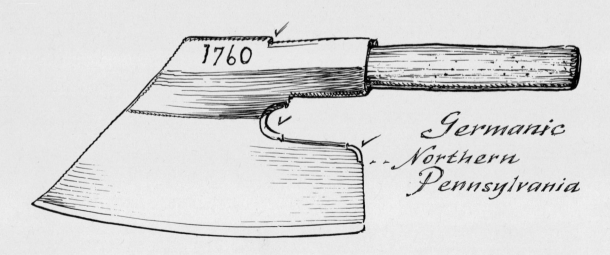

*Germanic
Northern
Pennsylvania*

but when they learned that it was only an old axe head, they felt as if they had been hoaxed. How, after all, could an axe head be considered a work of art!

The Civil War period marked a turning point in tool design, as it did for so much Americana. Before that time, the word tool meant an implement that could make one thing at a time; mass-production tools then entered the scene, and the word tool, which had meant only "hand tool," took on many added meanings. Finally the word tool came to mean any item having to do with the production of an item; it could be the machine and also the building that housed the machine. Even the salesmen, the advertising gadgets, and the business offices are "tools of the trade."

Generally speaking, hand tools made after the Civil War period lacked the simple beauty of those of the ante-bellum period. Things were made to sell quickly, things were made in large quantities so that they could be catalogued identically, and hand-made implements began to disappear. Wooden handles became "fancier," more curved and ornamental, but the severe beauty of folk art and primitive usage was lost. Saw handles became "trickier"; they were designed to appeal to the eye instead of to fit the hand. Axe handles, which had always been almost straight, as a good club should be, took on curves such as the "fawn foot" and the "scroll knob." By 1885, handles on axes and adzes had become almost too curved, but by the 1900's they settled down to a sensible and standard design, such as that of those you can buy now at the hardware store.

Before the Civil War, most axe handles (like the handles of all tools) were made by the man who would use the axe. A pattern was cut from a piece of flat wood and saved as the model from which future handles would be fashioned. Axe patterns (which you can still find in old barns) were so subtly curved and proportioned that they were as distinctive as a man's signature; you could take one look and say "This tool belongs to Jones" or "That tool belongs to Smith." Very often an axe-handle pattern was handed down from generation to generation, and it was considered counterfeit for another family to copy it.

While we are on the subject of the handles of old tools, I would like to point out that the collector should understand something of the philosophy about the connection between the workman's hand and that part of a hand tool that he touches. Most modern workmen will scoff at the idea, but any fine craftsman will tell you that the right wooden handle (let us say, on a hammer) helps you along with your work. A metal or plastic handle or even an incorrect wooden handle can feel "dead" and not "spring back" against pressure, thus causing blisters and slowing your work. The proper handle's "feel" or "heft" is the unexplainable quality that a fine violin has to the musician. *The Oxford History of Technology* quotes Christian Barman's comments on an exhibition of early hand tools: "Everybody who appreciates the qualities of materials loves wood, and here was wood formed into a special kind of tactile sculpture made to be felt with the hand. I remembered that old craftsmen, when they buy a new set of modern chisels, throw away the handles and carefully fit their own. These handles, polished bright by a lifetime of use, became part of their owners' lives."

Always in the fine art of working with wood, the old-time craftsman's laboratory was in his head and his hands and his heart. He called it "knack"; some now believe it was a "sixth sense" or an extrasensory power. Elusive as this "knack" may be, it is the most important part of those small differences that distinguish the master craftsman from the good workman.

When we consider tools, we are dealing with human benefactors of the most primary sort. Tools increase and vary human power; they economize human time, and they convert raw substances into valuable and useful products. So when we muse on historic tools as symbols, we are always analyzing the romance of human progress.

Although Early American tools were traditional in design to such an extent that one can usually tell the nationality of the maker, there are almost always subtle differences and decorative touches in design that equally identify the region of American countryside from which the tool came. A collector can easily tell a piece coming from Pennsylvania from one originating in Connecticut. This distinctiveness was often intentional; the Early American's urge for identification was born of pride both in himself and in his time. An extraordinary awareness of life and time permeated our early days; when something was made and the maker was satisfied, it wasn't complete until his mark and the date were added.

Nowadays things are almost obsolete before they leave the drawing board. How lucky we are that so many of the old tools and the things that were made with them were dated and touched with the craftsman's art.

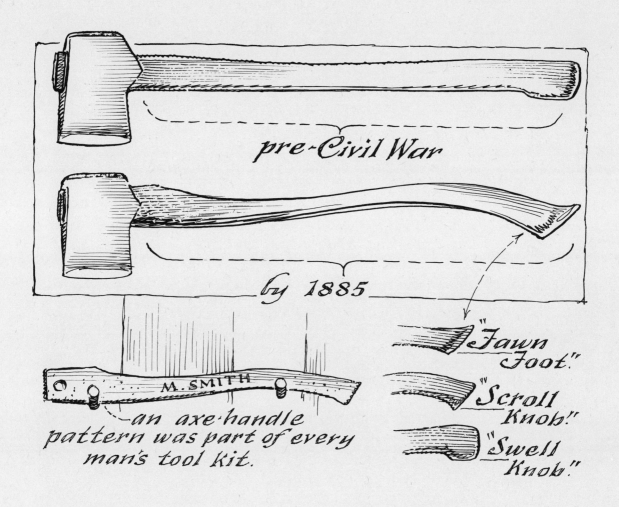

pre-Civil War

by 1885

"Fawn Foot."

"Scroll Knob."

"Swell Knob."

an axe-handle pattern was part of every man's tool kit.

M. SMITH

Crude Shops, Magnificent Results.

After the Civil War, factory-made things became popular and the tool house was limited to such minor work as farm repairs. The Dominy Shop (shown below) was used by Nathaniel Dominy IV (1737–1812) and his son Nathaniel V (1770–1852). This entire shop, including manuscript accounts covering the period from 1762 until 1829, has been kept intact at the Henry Francis du Pont Winterthur Museum in Delaware. The visitor's first reaction is usually "What a primitive shop!" Yet the magnificent table standing in the center of the room was made in it.

Courtesy, Henry Francis du Pont Winterthur Museum

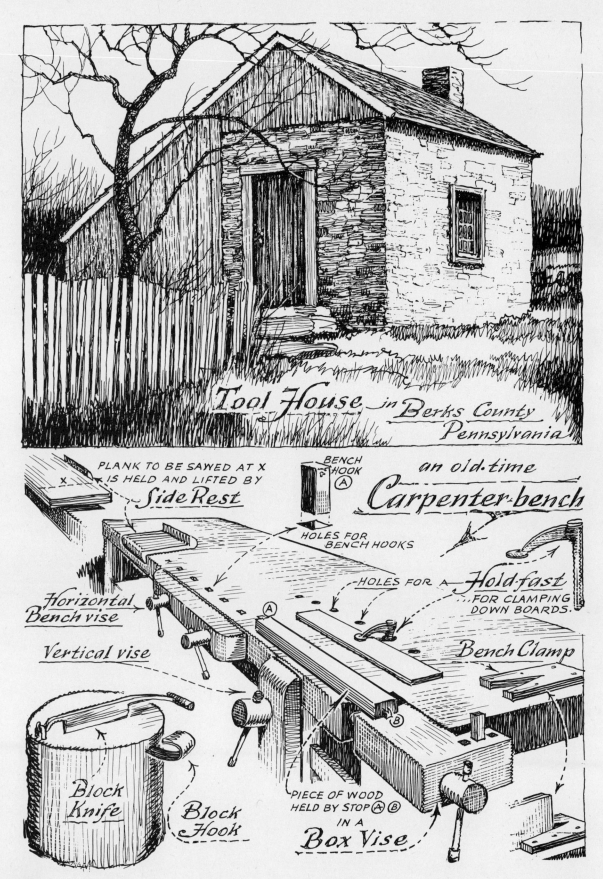

Tool House in Berks County Pennsylvania

PLANK TO BE SAWED AT X IS HELD AND LIFTED BY *Side Rest*

BENCH HOOK Ⓐ

an old-time *Carpenter-bench*

HOLES FOR BENCH HOOKS

HOLES FOR A *Hold-fast* FOR CLAMPING DOWN BOARDS.

Horizontal Bench vise

Vertical vise

Ⓐ

Bench Clamp

Ⓑ

Block Knife

Block Hook

PIECE OF WOOD HELD BY STOP Ⓐ Ⓑ IN A *Box Vise*

9

An Ax is an Axe!

No matter how you spell it (both ways are correct), it is natural to start off a sketchbook of Early American implements with this tool. America was a new world of unending wood where a man armed with only a felling axe could enter the forest and survive. With his axe he could clear the land of trees, cut fuel, build a bridge, a house, and furniture. With his axe he could fashion snares for game and, in a pinch, use it to protect himself against marauding Indians or wild beasts. No wonder the first settlers carried axes in their belts and treated them with a respect like that of a soldier toward his sword or side arms.

As was true of all first American artifacts, our earliest axes were like those from abroad. They had well-curved, gracefully fashioned blades, and they lacked the bulky polls such as those that identify the pure American design. The heavy poll appears to be for hammering (indeed it could have been used for such), yet it was devised to serve as a weight to give more momentum to chopping. Few early polless axes have survived except those traded with the Indians (trade axes).

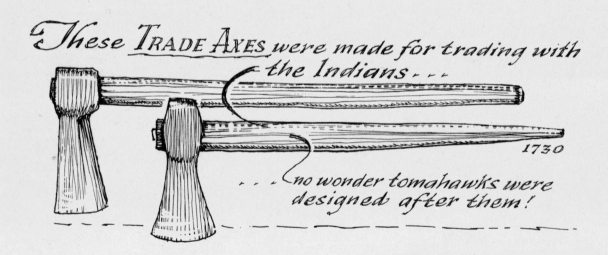

These TRADE AXES were made for trading with the Indians...

1730

...no wonder tomahawks were designed after them!

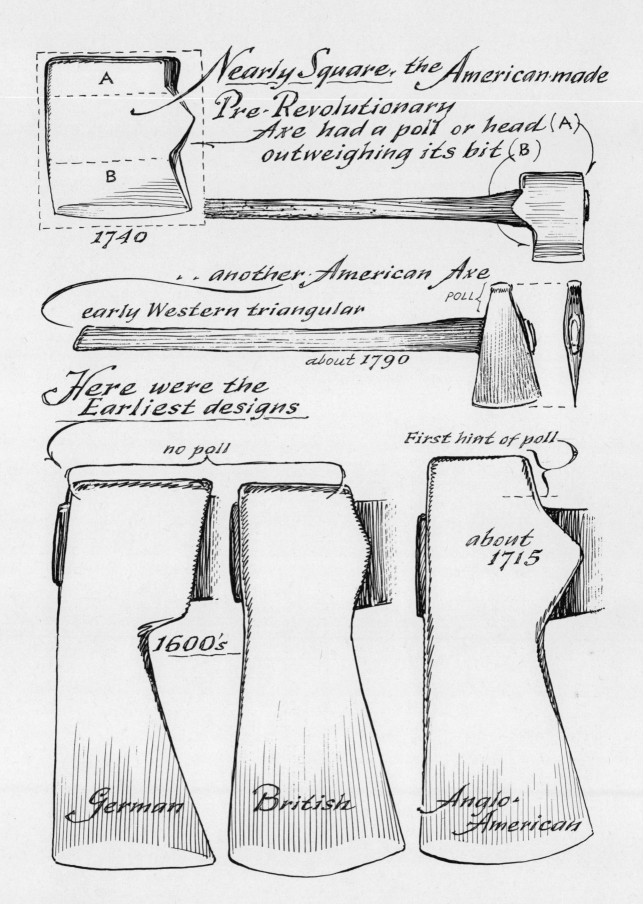

Nearly Square, the American-made *Pre-Revolutionary* Axe had a poll or head (A) outweighing its bit (B)

1740

... another American Axe

early Western triangular

POLL

about 1790

Here were the Earliest designs

no poll

First hint of poll

about 1715

1600's

German

British

Anglo-American

A World of Axes

America's wealth of wood and her pride in carpenter craftsmanship resulted in an amazing array of specialty tools. Early catalogues listed more than fifty patterns of axe heads alone, all doing the same jobs yet differing in design. Farmers and blacksmiths fashioned their own axes for framing and for mortising the beams of barns (shown below) or for felling trees (shown opposite).

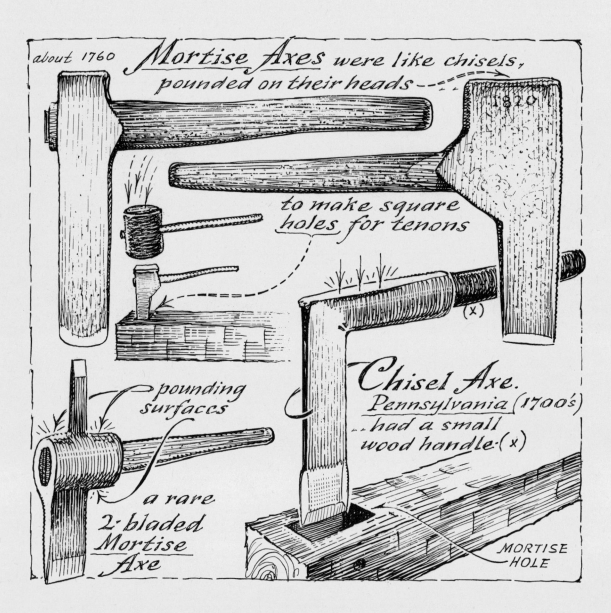

about 1760

Mortise Axes were like chisels, pounded on their heads --

1820

to make square holes for tenons

pounding surfaces

a rare 2-bladed Mortise Axe

Chisel Axe. Pennsylvania (1700's) .. had a small wood handle·(x)

(x)

MORTISE HOLE

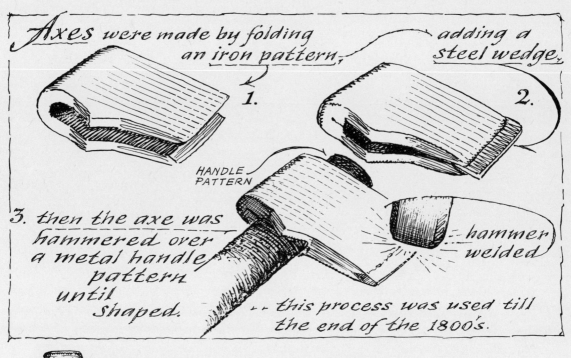

Axes were made by folding an iron pattern, adding a **steel wedge.**

1.

2.

HANDLE PATTERN

3. then the axe was hammered over a metal handle, pattern until Shaped.

-- hammer welded

-- this process was used till the end of the 1800's.

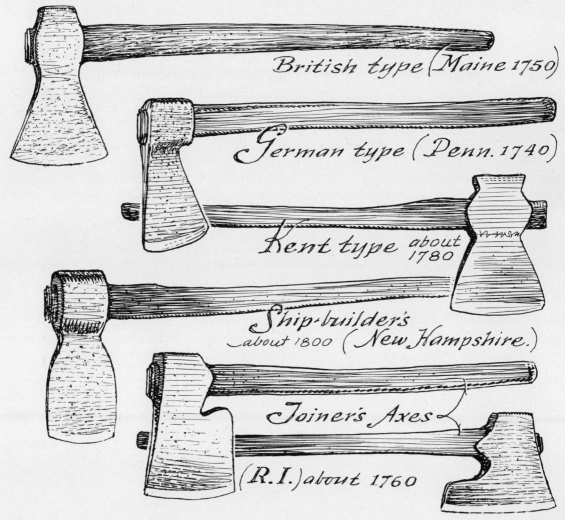

British type (Maine 1750)

German type (Penn. 1740)

Kent type about 1780

Ship-builder's about 1800 (New Hampshire.)

Joiner's Axes

(R.I.) about 1760

13

The Broad Axe.

A most essential Early American tool was the chisel-edged broad axe. Thousands of them are still around, but people seeing this broad axe often take it for a very big and clumsy felling axe. Because few museums bother either to include the tool or to explain its use, few people really know how it was used. Actually, it was a kind of plane or striking chisel that early Americans used for hewing round logs into square beams.

More than twice the size of a felling axe, this tool had a short bent handle protruding outward from the side of the axe head with the bevel (basil or chisel-slant) on that same side. Two hands were used; the process was called "squaring" or "hewing."

The American-style broad axe had a fair-sized squarish head, or poll (as the other American-style axes did); European types had none.

Although hand-hewn timbers in old buildings are commonly called "adzed beams," they were usually broad-axed.

Although some odd people hack up beams "to make them appear hand done," the most expert broad-axe man cut the fewest axe marks, and those that were left were spaced nicely—never haphazardly.

Never haphazard!

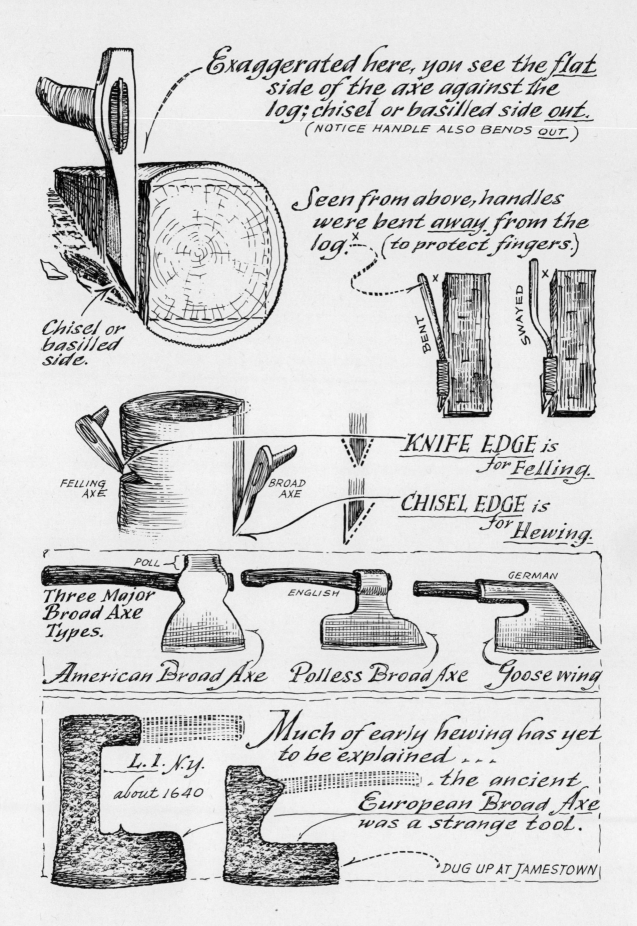

Exaggerated here, you see the flat side of the axe against the log; chisel or basilled side out.
(NOTICE HANDLE ALSO BENDS OUT.)

Chisel or basilled side.

Seen from above, handles were bent away from the log. (to protect fingers.)

BENT

SWAYED

FELLING AXE

BROAD AXE

KNIFE EDGE is for Felling.

CHISEL EDGE is for Hewing.

Three Major Broad Axe Types.

POLL

ENGLISH

GERMAN

American Broad Axe   Polless Broad Axe   Goosewing

L.I. N.Y. about 1640

Much of early hewing has yet to be explained ... the ancient European Broad Axe was a strange tool.

DUG UP AT JAMESTOWN

How the Broad Axe was Used.

Any old-timer is willing to tell you how to use a broad axe, but each one is bound to describe a different method. Trying to ferret out the truth I asked everyone who visited my collection—if the visitor claimed he knew the art—to demonstrate broad-axing. Some "used to stand upon the log, hewing as they walked along it." "But you wouldn't be able to reach the log with so short a handle! You'd chop your toes off!" was my reply. But they insisted, and offered to demonstrate. The doctor managed to sew one toe back on very nicely.

Actually, a walk-along-the-log method was used, but with a special broad axe unlike the ancient ones with bent handles. (This is shown on the following page.) As for the ancient chisel-edged broad axe, you walked *alongside* the log, working as you went. One man would swing horizontally (with the grain); another would hit straight downward; another would strike at an angle. As for me, I contend there was no generally accepted procedure. Mercer (in *Ancient Carpenters' Tools*) says that the broad axe was usually "held with both hands, right hand foremost. The leg face was set against the workman's left side and he hewed with both hands, not longways with the grain but diagonally *downward* across it."

DOGS" were used to fasten logs to be worked upon.

two types

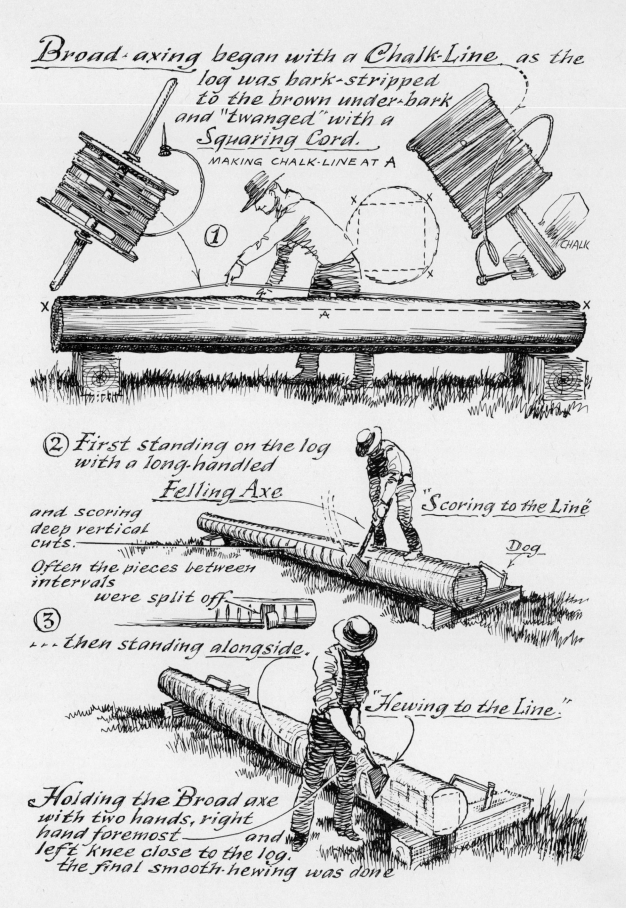

Broad-axing began with a *Chalk-Line*, as the log was bark-stripped to the brown under-bark and "twanged" with a *Squaring Cord.*

MAKING CHALK-LINE AT A

CHALK

①

② *First standing on the log with a long-handled*

Felling Axe

"Scoring to the Line"

and scoring deep vertical cuts.

Often the pieces between intervals were split off.

Dog

③

...then standing alongside.

"Hewing to the Line."

Holding the Broad axe with two hands, right hand foremost and left knee close to the log, the final smooth-hewing was done

A Giant and a Midget.

The straight-handled broad axe—a knife-edged axe beveled on both sides —was usually used to hew railroad ties. Logging railroads that make their ties out of softwood hew just two sides of the log. A tree was felled at a slight angle (held at one end by its own branches), and the hewer walked first up and then down, flattening the sides as he went. The same axe was used both for scoring and hewing! This process seems difficult but it was fast.

Because this axe has a straight handle, it is often mistaken for some re-handled ancient broad axe, ground on two sides to convert it into a felling axe. The only clue to its true use is that its ponderous head is much too heavy to swing sideways as an axe must be swung in felling.

The smallest version of the hewing axe is the carpenter's hewing hatchet (below). It sometimes looks like a toy model of the big one. Never used to split wood or to drive nails, these hatchets were used for shaping.

a tiny *Carpenter's Hewing Hatchet*

about 1725

side view.

3 1/4"

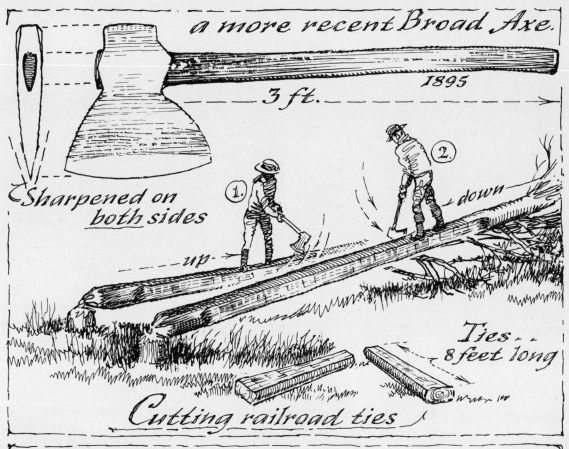

a more recent Broad Axe.

1895

3 ft.

Sharpened on both sides

1. up

2. down

Ties... 8 feet long

Cutting railroad ties

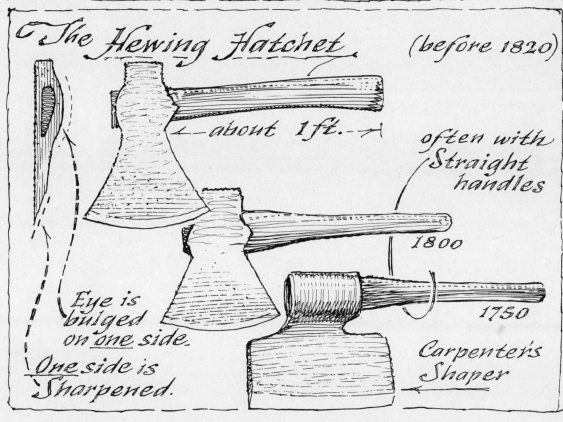

The Hewing Hatchet   (before 1820)

about 1 ft.

often with Straight handles

1800

Eye is bulged on one side.

One side is Sharpened.

1750

Carpenter's Shaper

The Hatchet.

Today's household hatchet began as the "shingling hatchet." This had a flared shape with slightly rounded nail-hammering head and a nail-pulling notch in the bit. Because the first New World roofs were thatched, shingling hatchets were unknown to the early settler. Shingling hatchets so often fell from roofs being worked on that roofers frequently had them strung for hanging at the wrist.

The "lathing hatchet" is recognized by its flat outside contour, made so nails could be struck near a ceiling without hitting it. If the axe head flared, the flare was on the inside of the bit. It soon became the favorite carpenter's tool to replace the awkward cooper's hatchet. (See opposite. The cooper rounding off a barrel head is using a cooper's hatchet; notice how it was held close to its head rather than by the end of its handle.)

The 1790 American axe-hatchet (shown below) was a miniature model of the square-headed American axe with the poll that outweighed the bit.

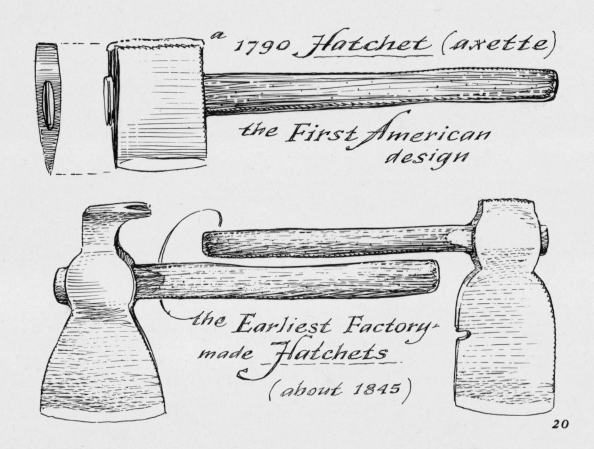

a 1790 *Hatchet (axette)*

the *First American design*

the *Earliest Factory-made Hatchets*

(about 1845)

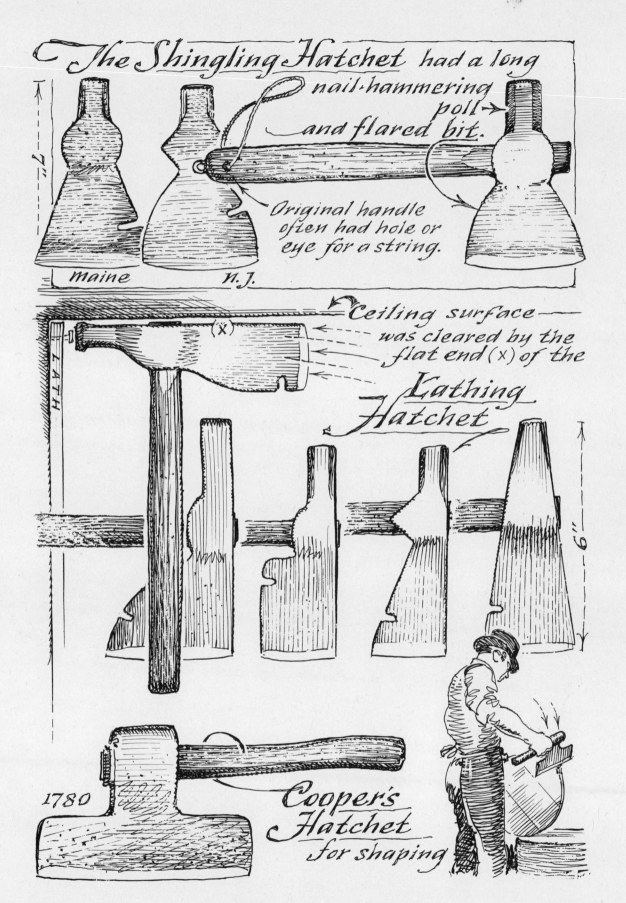

The *Shingling Hatchet* had a long
nail-hammering
poll →
and flared bit.

7"

*Original handle
often had hole or
eye for a string.*

maine   n.j.

↱ Ceiling surface
was cleared by the
flat end (x) of the

Lathing
Hatchet

(x)

LATH

6"

1780

Cooper's
Hatchet
for shaping

21

Hammers

The claw hammer hasn't changed much since about 75 A.D. Aside from its aesthetic qualities, the Roman example shown below has a most efficient design (which might do well to show up any day now).

The use of nails in the 1600's and the 1700's was more efficient then than now. The early square-cut nails, for instance, had greater holding power than our round nails; furthermore, they retarded splitting of the wood. The practice of "clinching" (bending over the protruding point) is now regarded as poor workmanship, but its efficiency is obvious. Early batten doors with wrought nails on the outside and bent points on the inside are cemented together so well that it is next to impossible to pry them apart.

Perhaps the rarity of ancient iron hammers in America is due to the once widespread practice of using wooden mallets to drive in wooden nails (tree-nails or trunnels), even wooden nails of a tiny toothpick size. Wooden mallets were also used as striking chisels; iron hammers, *only* for metal nails.

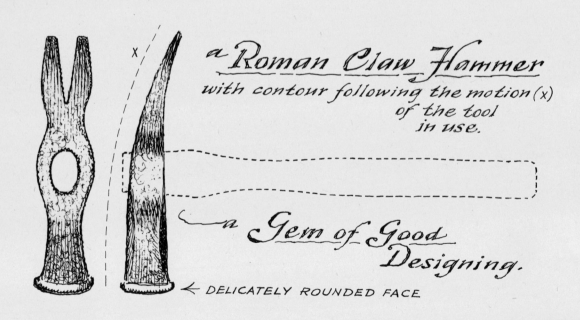

x

a Roman Claw Hammer
with contour following the motion (x) of the tool in use.

a Gem of Good Designing.

← DELICATELY ROUNDED FACE

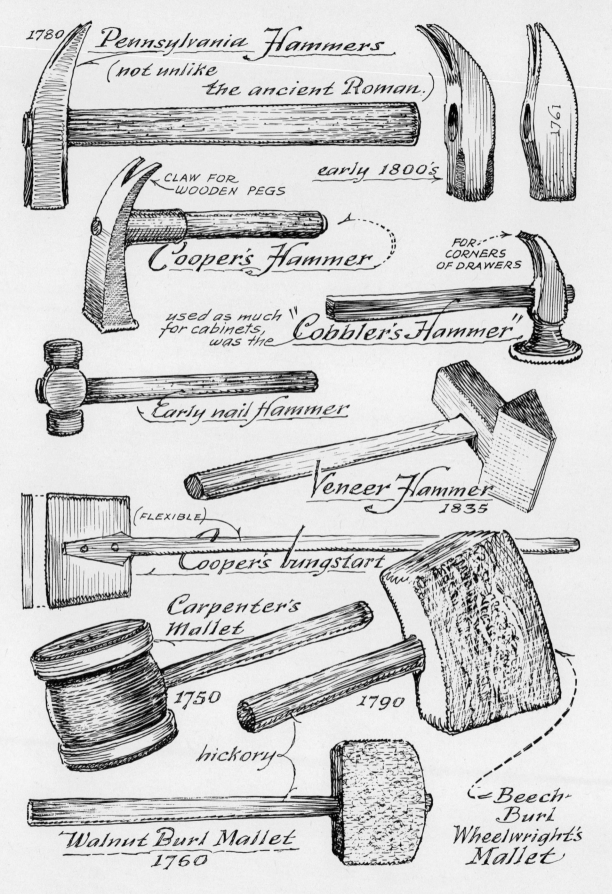

1780

Pennsylvania Hammers

(not unlike the ancient Roman.)

early 1800's

1761

CLAW FOR WOODEN PEGS

Cooper's Hammer

FOR CORNERS OF DRAWERS

used as much for cabinets, was the "Cobbler's Hammer"

Early nail Hammer

Veneer Hammer
1835

(FLEXIBLE)

Cooper's bungstart

Carpenter's Mallet
1750

1790

hickory

Walnut Burl Mallet
1760

Beech-Burl Wheelwright's Mallet

The Axe and the Log House.

Before we leave the subject of axes, the reader will be interested in seeing just what was expected of the axe. Here are some standard log-house notches often made with only the axe.

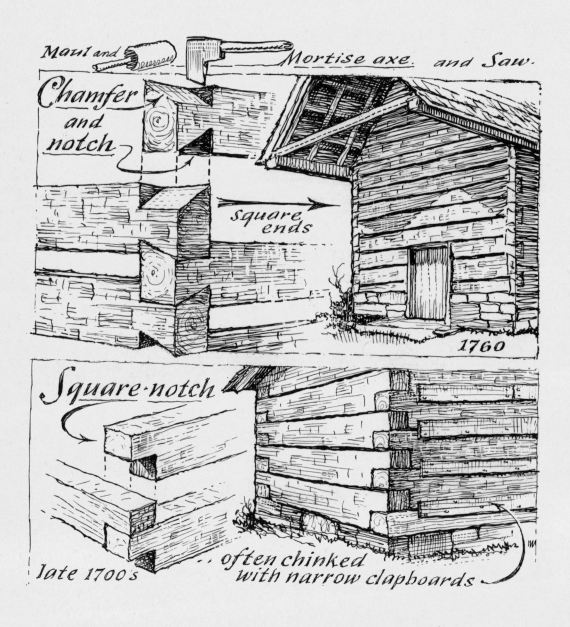

Maul and Mortise axe. and Saw.

Chamfer and notch

square ends

1760

Square·notch

late 1700's ... often chinked with narrow clapboards

Saddle·notch

1. Axe cut 2. Gutter Adze to round out

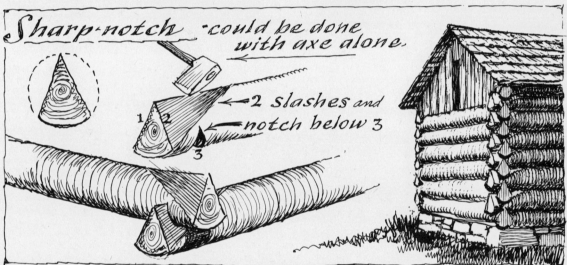

Sharp·notch — could be done with axe alone.

2 slashes and notch below 3

1 2 3

Dovetail·notch   came from Sweden (c.1640)

Lip adze and axe.

upper notch slants out to drain rain.

The Adze

The idea of a sharp tool with its blade at a right angle to the handle is most ancient. The Early American version was swung in the curvature of the blade, with the arm and tool forming the radius.

Because of its flaring square end, the adze head had to be removable (as the bevel to be sharpened was on the inside and inaccessible to a grindstone). Some of the earliest adzes, however, had nonremovable heads, which had to be sharpened with a whetstone.

The shipwright's adze had a long peg-poll for driving down broken nails (and to prevent the blade from being nicked).

As shown below, the right-angle cuts on old beams are make-ready scorings for broad-axe work, not so-called "adze marks." Only on special "parlor beams" (these were made to be exposed) was the adze introduced; then the surface effect was from a delicate ripple to almost complete smoothness.

The Adze made surfaces smooth

Broad-axed beam with make-ready axe scorings left showing.

---> it didn't leave score marks.

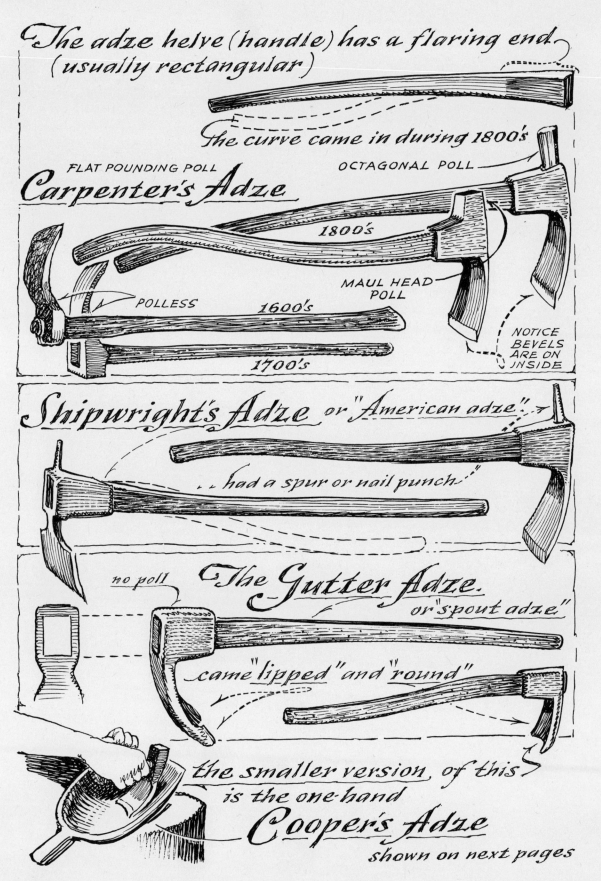

The adze helve (handle) has a flaring end.
(usually rectangular)

The curve came in during 1800's

FLAT POUNDING POLL   OCTAGONAL POLL

Carpenter's Adze

1800's

MAUL HEAD
POLL

POLLESS   1600's

1700's

NOTICE
BEVELS
ARE ON
INSIDE

Shipwright's Adze or "American adze"

...had a spur or nail punch...

no poll   **The Gutter Adze.**

or "spout adze."

came "lipped" and "round"

the smaller version of this
is the one-hand
Cooper's Adze

shown on next pages

Canoes and Bowls

The word canoe (canow and canoo in the 1600's) described a hollowed-out log. Until the Indians saw the English hand adze, they used fire to burn out the hollow portion and flint knives and shells to scrape out the burned wood. Then they devised their own adze, using flint instead of metal for the blade. The scoop, or scorp, became refined as the years went by, and, finally, it became a finishing tool.

Maple and ash burls (wartlike bumps on tree trunks) were first burned and then scorped out, making the toughest and most durable of all bowls.

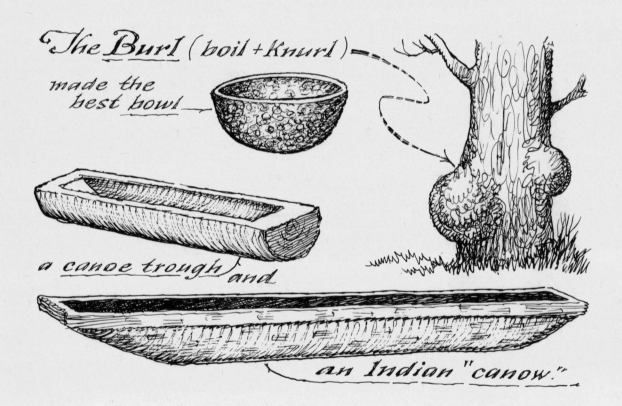

The Burl (boil + knurl) made the best bowl — a canoe trough and an Indian "canow."

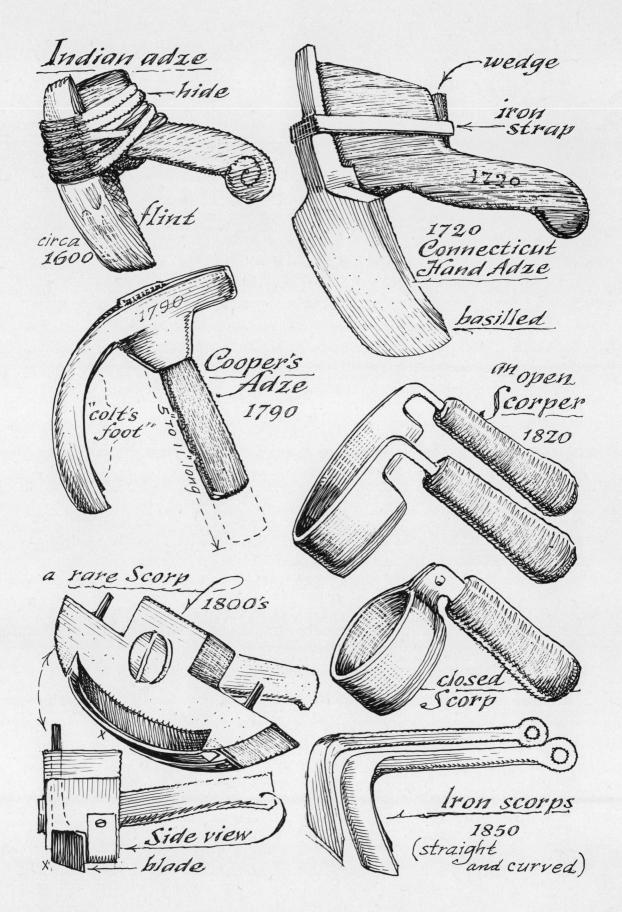

Indian adze
— hide
flint
circa 1600

wedge
iron strap
1720
1720 Connecticut Hand Adze
basilled

1790
Cooper's Adze 1790
"colt's foot"
5 to 11" long

an open Scorper 1820

a rare Scorp 1800's
Side view
blade

closed Scorp

Iron scorps 1850
(straight and curved)

Wedges and Froes

A good woodsman would never consider using his axe as a hammer to hit the head of a wedge. That would not only widen the eye but also would finally split the cheeks, finishing off the axe head forever. Yet many paintings of Lincoln show him splitting rails with an axe. Rails were split with wedges. Iron wedges (or wooden gluts) were driven into the wood with a heavy maul or beetle (as shown below).

To split shingles, laths, staves, and clapboards, a knife-type wedge called a froe or frow (shown on the opposite page) was struck with a short maul known as a froe-club. In England the froe is known also as a fromard or rending-axe. The clapboard-maker struck away from himself and twisted the froe handle to split the board with the grain, while striking away with the froe-club (see drawing).

The froe became obsolete about a century ago, when it became customary to saw-cut shingles and laths. Till then, "riving" shingles was a favorite rainy-day woodshed job, and every household had several froes on hand.

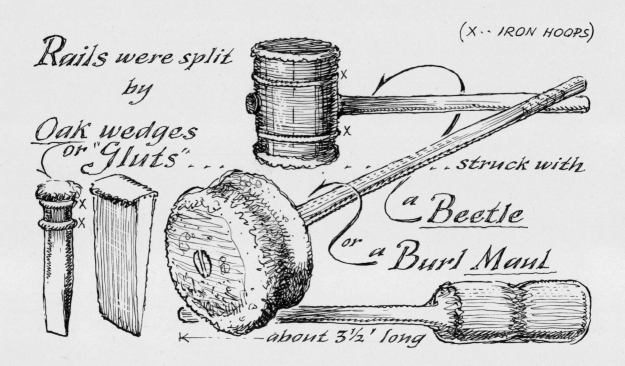

(X ·· IRON HOOPS)

Rails were split by

Oak wedges or "Gluts"........

........*struck with*

a Beetle

or a Burl Maul

←——— *about 3½' long*

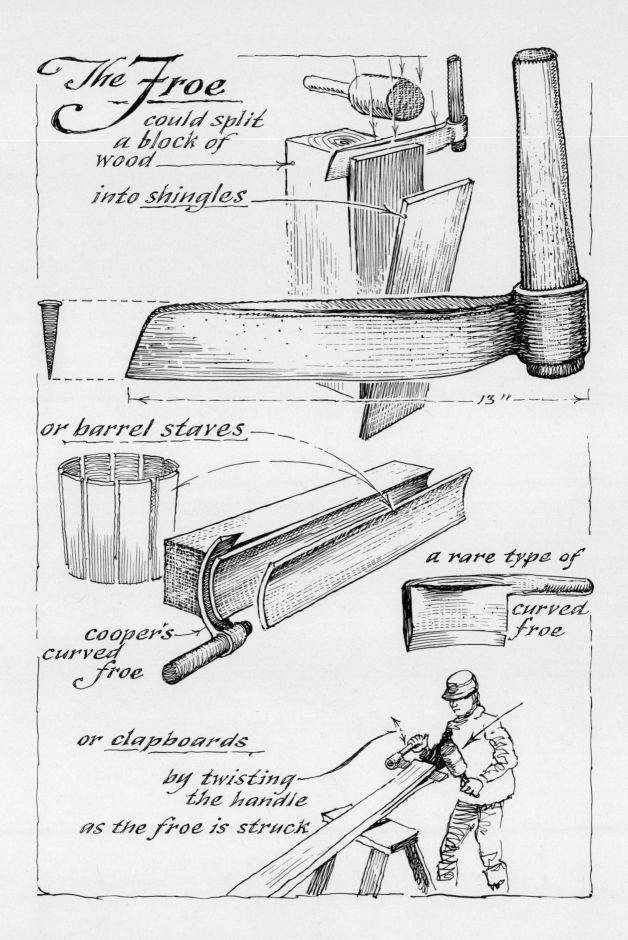

The Froe

could split
a block of
wood

into shingles

13"

or barrel staves

cooper's
curved
froe

a rare type of

curved
froe

or clapboards

by twisting
the handle
as the froe is struck

The Fine Art of Splitting

The uses of the froe were many. Very old men, too feeble to swing an axe, were given the chore of splitting kindling from logs. Half-round barrel hoops were also split with the froe. Willow poles were split in half for making gates and hurdles. The early hurdle was not like our horse hurdle; it was a section of fence that could be lashed to other similar sections to make a portable animal enclosure.

Lathing was split with the froe from fresh oak, in both single strips and "flats." Lath flats were split first on one side, then the other, making a sort of accordion piece that could be unfolded.

The saw was almost never used for cutting with the grain or lengthwise: splitting a length of wood was so much easier. A craftsman could split inch-square lengths from a large piece of wood in a fraction of the time that it would take him to saw them.

Because of the many uses of the froe, there is hardly an old barn left that doesn't have a number of these tools tucked away somewhere in it. Less ubiquitous, however, are their battered mates, the froe-clubs.

the Froe-Club
new

used

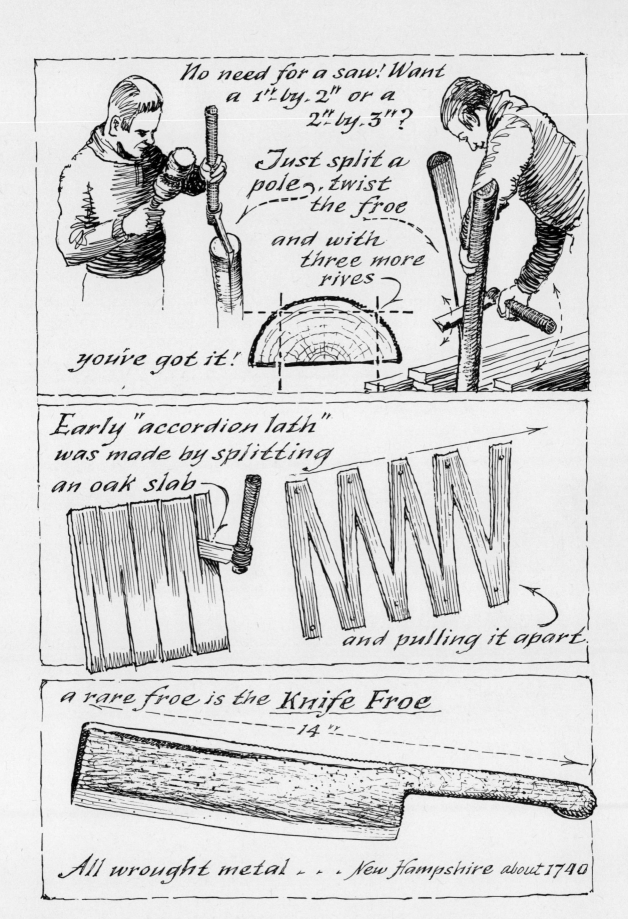

No need for a saw! Want a 1″ by 2″ or a 2″ by 3″?

Just split a pole, twist the froe

and with three more rives

you've got it!

Early "accordion lath" was made by splitting an oak slab

and pulling it apart.

a rare froe is the Knife Froe

14″

All wrought metal . . . New Hampshire about 1740

33

Tools with Legs

Chairmaking was one of the earliest industries of the Shakers, so it is natural that they were also pioneers in installing their wonderful mechanical appliances onto benches so that operators could sit while working. The first American shingle bench may have been made in Maine or Pennsylvania, but it reached its peak in design with the Shakers.

One Lebanon (New York) shinglemaker filled a request for 5,000 shingles in December of 1789, which, apparently, was a usual sort of output for one operator. Shaker-made broom-vices, apple parers, nail-benches, and herb-cutters were installed on legs and attached to stools of one kind or another or designed so that the buyer could affix the appliance to a bench he made himself. To sit at work was, all of a sudden, a new American pleasure.

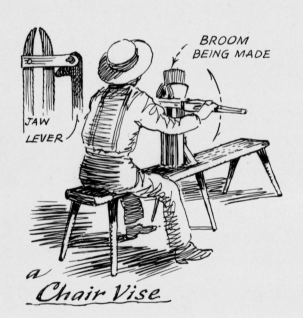

a *Chair Vise*

an *Apple Quarterer*

To Sit at your Work . . .

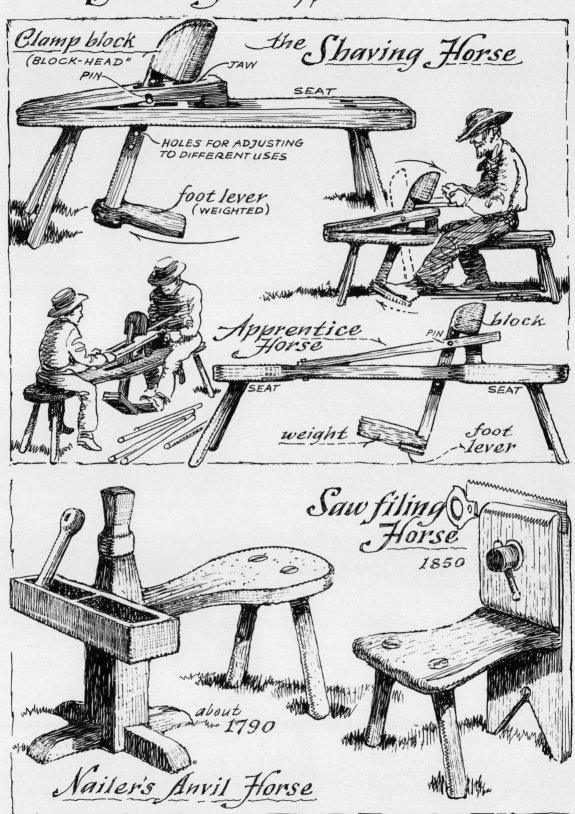

Clamp block
("BLOCK-HEAD"
PIN
JAW
SEAT

the **Shaving Horse**

HOLES FOR ADJUSTING
TO DIFFERENT USES

foot lever
(WEIGHTED)

Apprentice Horse

PIN   block

SEAT   SEAT

weight   foot lever

Saw filing Horse
1850

about 1790

Nailer's Anvil Horse

The American Horse

The American saw-horse is now usually carpenter-made and hastily knocked together by the workman to be discarded "after the job is done"; it can also be bought ready-made, put together with "two-by-fours" and metal fasteners. Either way the modern saw-horse is more a temporary prop than a well-designed table. The early saw-horse, which had a flat top, was wide enough to hold the wood being sawed and other things too; it was usually a handy and permanent part of the tool room.

An Early American sawyer's prop was made of two clubs pushed against a raised log. A later arrangement was the "tackle prop," a stick pushed through a forked bough; two of these could hold a whole log in place.

The first "saw-buck" was a tripod (a tilted cross with a stick through it) and it was called a "saw-goat" instead of a "saw-buck" (the Dutch word *zaag-boc* means saw-goat). So the three-legged *zaag-boc* became our four-legged saw-buck!

Zaag-boc to Saw-buck 1600's 1700's

"Saw-horses" were saw-tables

1750

for carpenters...

or when LOGS were to be sawed,
you used a Sawyer's Prop

made
of
two "clubs"

hole

or a Sawing Tackle

Single or double

"For Making "Snitzels""

First called the "drawing knife" because you drew it toward you, the drawknife (or snitzel-knife, as some Pennsylvanians called it) came to America before the Pilgrims. But only with the emergence of the snitzel-bank, or shaving horse, which made it simpler to hold the article being shaved, did the drawknife become a most favored tool. There are probably more ancient drawknives extant than any other antique tool.

The drawknife was used to taper the sides of shingles, to rough-size the edges of floor boards and rough-trim paneling before planing them, to fashion axe, rake, and other tool handles, and to make stool legs, ox yokes, pump handles, and wheel spokes. It is easy to see why the drawknife was so popular! The final finishing on much drawknife work was done by our next tool, the spokeshave and scraper.

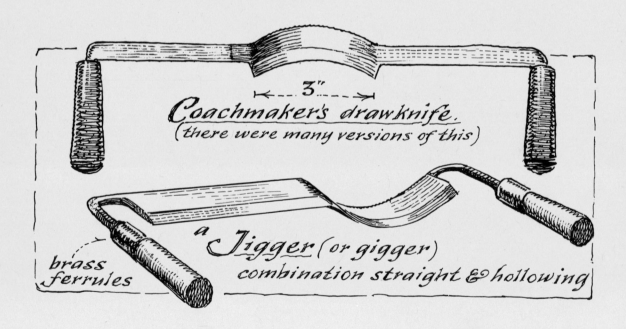

3"
Coachmaker's drawknife.
(there were many versions of this)

a Jigger (or gigger)
combination straight & hollowing

brass ferrules

The Drawknife *first called Draft Shave*
ranged from the 24" Mast Drawknife

1840

to the 6" bladed Cooper's Drawknife.

bent-over tines to secure the handles.

about 1700

Drawknife work was done on the Shaving Horse
.. the piece worked on clamped by the "Jaw"

.. or done on a Shaving Block, the piece held by a block hook (and the worker's body x)

STAVE

. . . . or for bench work. a Screw cramp

Hollow shave

Little Shavers and Big

The difference between the drawknife and its little brother the spokeshave is like the difference between the old open razor and the safety razor. The spokeshave has a regulated depth of cut. Tap the tangs and the cut deepens; tap the face of the blade back and it becomes more shallow. Often a screw held the adjustment in place. All-metal spokeshaves appeared just before the Civil War; before that, the variety of wood handles seems endless.

The biggest shaver was the chamfer knife, sometimes all metal, which is often misrepresented (even by the experts) as a kind of froe. The sharp upper surface, however, shows that it was not designed for striking; and the curve-beveled blade is certainly not for splitting.

Although the tiny tools shown below were called "top and side shaves," they were really planes. They were designed for the use of stair-makers, but coachmakers found them even more useful.

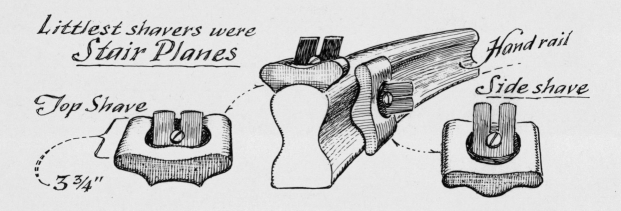

Littlest shavers were
Stair Planes

Top Shave

3¾"

Hand rail

Side shave

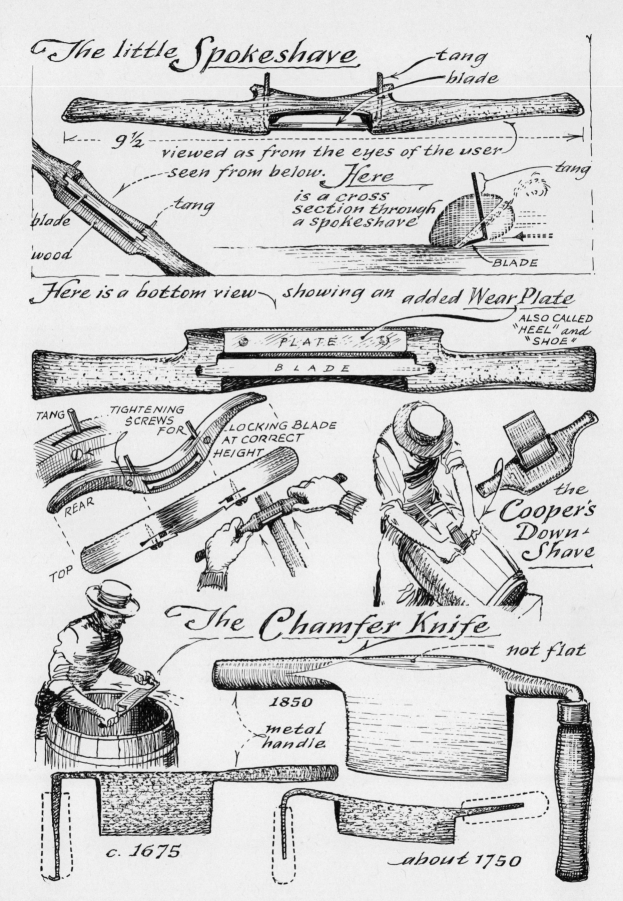

The little **Spokeshave**

tang
blade

9½

viewed as from the eyes of the user

seen from below. *Here* is a cross section through a spokeshave

blade
wood
tang

BLADE
tang

Here is a bottom view showing an added *Wear Plate*

ALSO CALLED "HEEL" and "SHOE"

PLATE
BLADE

TANG
TIGHTENING SCREWS FOR

LOCKING BLADE AT CORRECT HEIGHT

REAR
TOP

the Cooper's Down-Shave

The Chamfer Knife

not flat

1850
metal handle

c. 1675

about 1750

41

The Days of River Rafting.

In many wooded areas of eighteenth-century America, farmers raised crops mostly for their own use and derived cash only from the sale of wood. Timber was floated to its destination by means of fastening logs into giant rafts. Three or more "platforms" were fastened, one behind the other, to make one long raft; steering was done by long oars. When rafts were sold and dismantled at the mill, irons and fastening devices were put into kegs, loaded on wagons, and hauled back to the farm. Most farmers ran at least one raft a year in late winter (when rivers were high) and busied themselves a good part of each winter with making or repairing lumbering implements.

White pine for masts and spars was a prime American export in the early 1800's and up until the Civil War. On such rivers as the Delaware were floated more than a thousand rafts each spring. The largest one on record was 215 feet long, and it contained 120,000 feet of lumber.

Below is a device known as a "bow-and-pin fastener." The square pins were driven into holes in the log; the wooden bow held the lash pole in place.

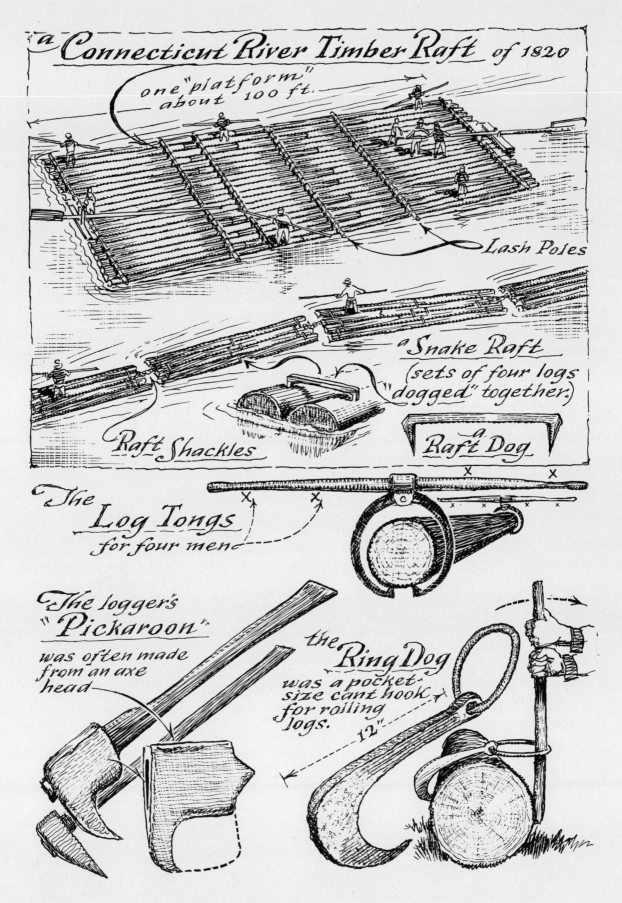

a Connecticut River Timber Raft of 1820

one "platform" about 100 ft.

Lash Poles

"Snake Raft (sets of four logs "dogged" together.)

Raft Shackles

a Raft Dog

The Log Tongs for four men

"The logger's "Pickaroon" was often made from an axe head

the Ring Dog was a pocket-size cant hook for rolling logs.

12"

Tools of the River Lumberman

*The American word "lumberman" came before our present
use of the word lumber. "Lumber" at one time (and still does in England)
meant "anything useless or cumbersome."*

The so-called "ship augers" you find in antique shops had not, as you
might think, anything to do with ships; they were really used for log-
rafts, or log-ships. The length of these augers allowed a man to bore a
hole while standing.

The lash-pole and wooden-pin method of building rafts was later re-
placed by iron raft shackles and "dogs."

Loose logs were "herded" into "corrals" by the owners at the mill
(branded with the owners' marks). The marking axe was also an inspec-
tion axe with a special bark-lifting poll.

Below you may see how the cant hook was made (in 1870 by a blacksmith named John Peavey) into the "American peavey" by wedding it to
the jam pike. The jam pike pried, the cant hook rolled, but the peavey
did both.

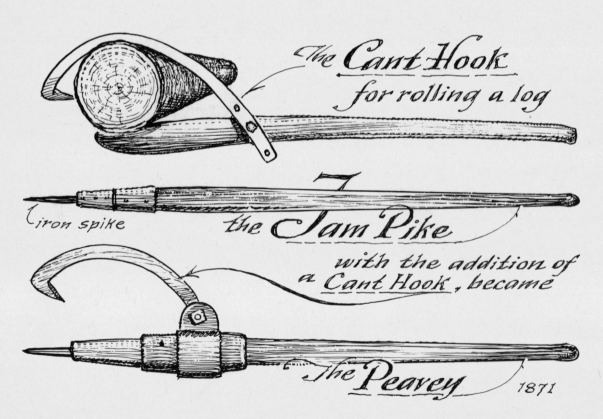

The *Cant Hook*
for rolling a log

iron spike   the *Jam Pike*

with the addition of
a *Cant Hook*, became

The *Peavey*   1871

44

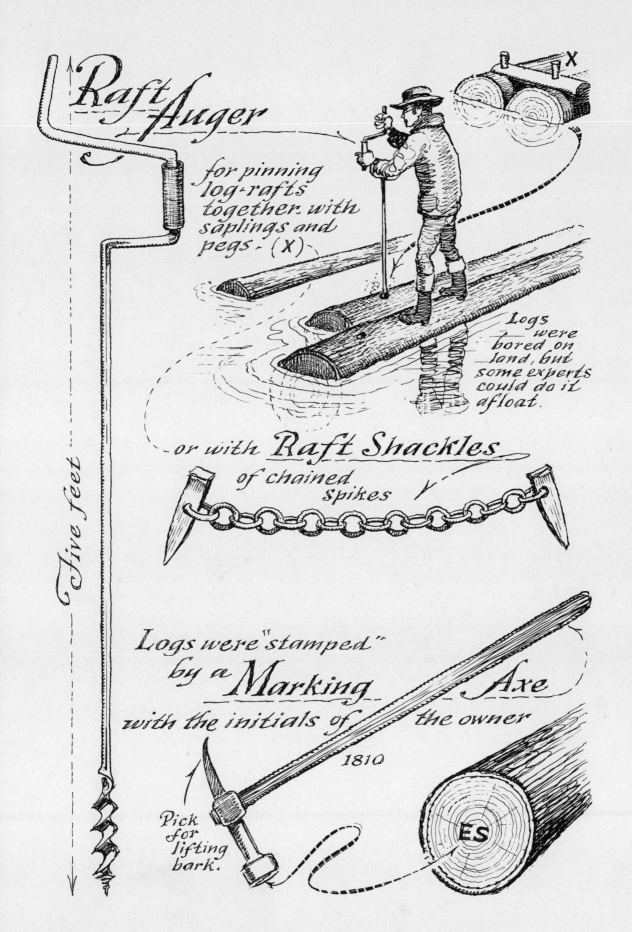

Raft Auger

for pinning
log-rafts
together with
saplings and
pegs - (X)

Logs
were
bored on
land, but
some experts
could do it
afloat.

Five feet

or with **Raft Shackles**

of chained
spikes

Logs were "stamped"
by a **Marking**   **Axe**

with the initials of   the owner

1810

Pick
for
lifting
bark.

ES

X

Of Cider and Apple Butter

Anything that touched apples, according to the old way of thinking, had to be made of wood. Even a nail would "risk spoiling the flavor" or "quicken a souring." So heavy treen-ware (appliances and tools made from trees) was necessary in the apple industry.

Cider was never a matter of just squeezing—there was a special art to "bruising" apples and leaving them exposed to air for a certain and exact time before pressing. Oddly, those who picked eating apples carefully from the tree to avoid bumping them made an elaborate ceremony of crushing the same fruit when making cider.

Apples were never squeezed: "pomace was pressed." A mash was made into pomace or "cheese," then carefully placed between straw mats so the juice could be pressed out. The pomace rake, apple butter scoop, "cheese cutter," and apple shovel are tools that are difficult to understand now, for they are lost to the times when cider was America's national drink and apple butter the national spread.

Apple butter Scoop 1790

Combination Scoop and paddle (both Shaker)

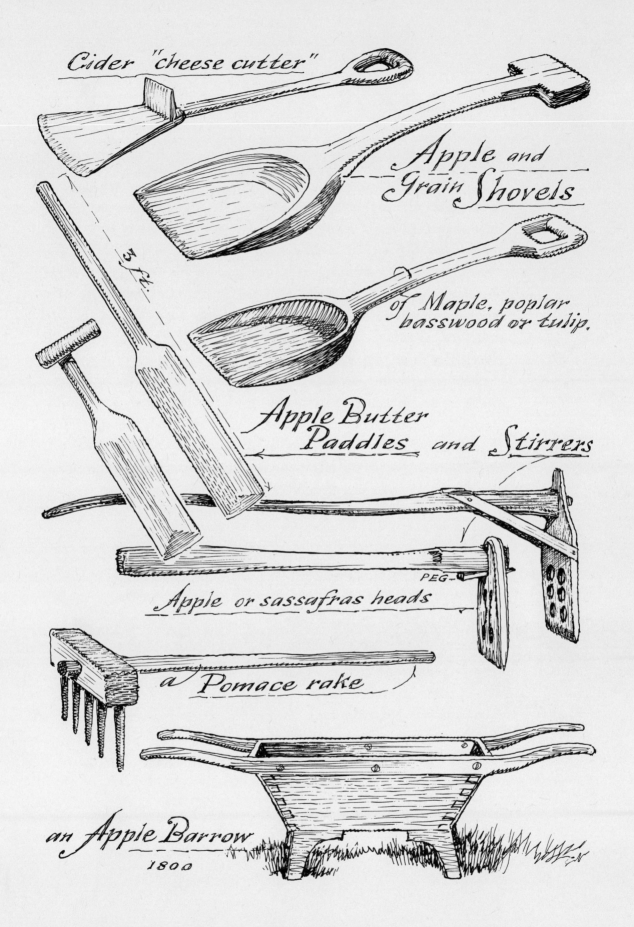

Cider "cheese cutter"

Apple and Grain Shovels

3 ft.

of Maple, poplar basswood or tulip.

Apple Butter Paddles and Stirrers

PEG

Apple or sassafras heads

a Pomace rake

an Apple Barrow
1800

47

To Remove Bark

Until recently the main source of tannin for treating hides was obtained from oak bark, and the production of oak bark was an essential part of the economy of many American farms. In April and May, bark peeled easily, and this was done with the spud, barking iron, and barking axe. The peeling chisel and adze were used mostly for "debarking" cedar posts and cleaning logs before broad-axing. The irons and spuds were true tanbark tools, usually blacksmith-made to order.

At first, chunks of oak bark were ground under massive stone mill wheels that turned into a trough of stone, but as early as 1797 the iron bark mill entered the scene to create a major American industry.

The liquor for tanning was obtained by pouring cold water on finely ground bark and leaving it to stand for a few days. Then it was passed from one leaching pit to another till the desired strength was reached.

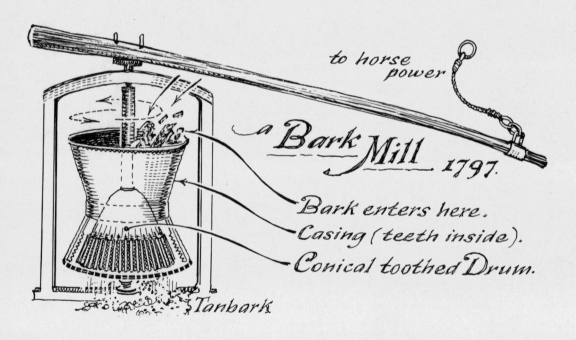

to horse power

a Bark Mill 1797.

Bark enters here.
Casing (teeth inside).
Conical toothed Drum.

Tanbark

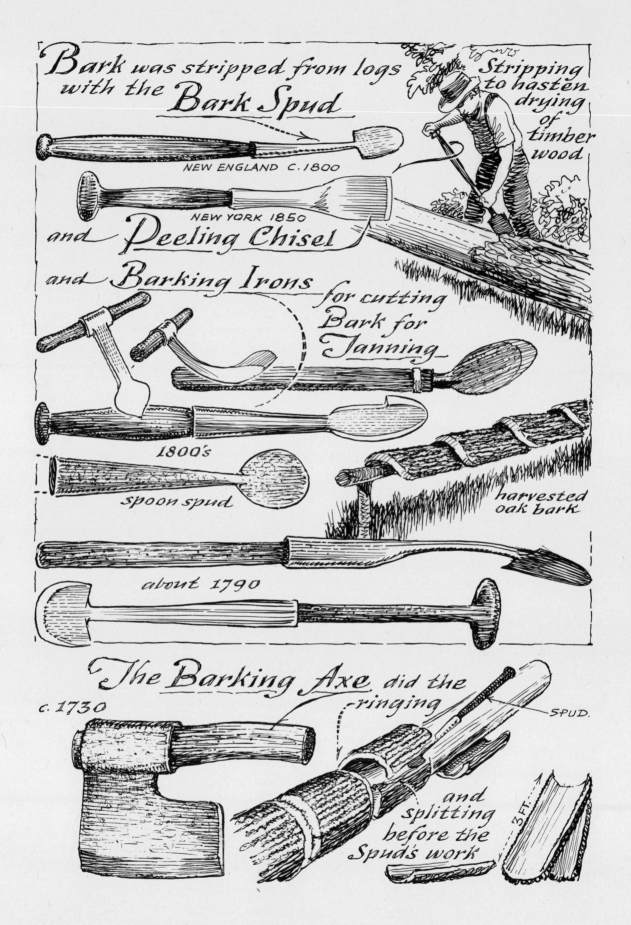

Bark was stripped from logs
with the **Bark Spud**

Stripping to hasten drying of timber wood

NEW ENGLAND C. 1800

NEW YORK 1850

and **Peeling Chisel**

and **Barking Irons**

for cutting Bark for Tanning

1800's

spoon spud

harvested oak bark

about 1790

The **Barking Axe** did the ringing

c. 1730

SPUD.

and splitting before the Spud's work

3 FT.

Two Heads are Better than One.

Except for the double-bitted axe, these tools are rare. So rare in fact, that there is doubt about their true names. One of the first dictionary mentions of the "twibil" calls it "an iron tool used by Paviers" (road-builders). This would make it a sort of grubbing hoe. Another describes it as a twin-billed hoe-and-knife for beans and peas. One old dictionary says the "twivel" is "among Carpenters, a tool to make Tortoise Holes." We must assume this definition was dictated to a printer who mistook "mortise" for "tortoise."

I would guess that all two-bitted hatchets might have been at some time called "twin-bills," "twibils," or "twivels." Still used in England to cut hurdle mortises, the twivel there is called "tomyhawk," "dader," or "two-bill."

The ice hatchet, adze-hatchet, and hatchet-adze were American, but only the Yankee double-bit remains. From Maine (about 1840) it was designed with one razor-sharp bit that could do fine work and one less sharp for rough work. It also provides a means for being held (by sinking it into a stump) for filing either bit.

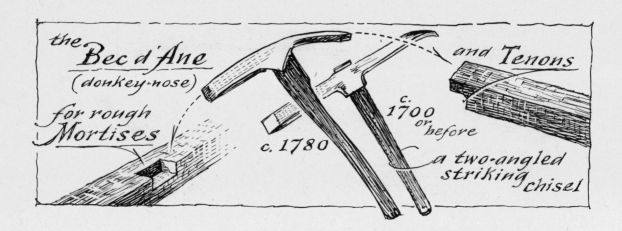

the Bec d'Ane (donkey-nose) for rough Mortises c. 1780 c. 1700 or before and Tenons a two-angled striking chisel

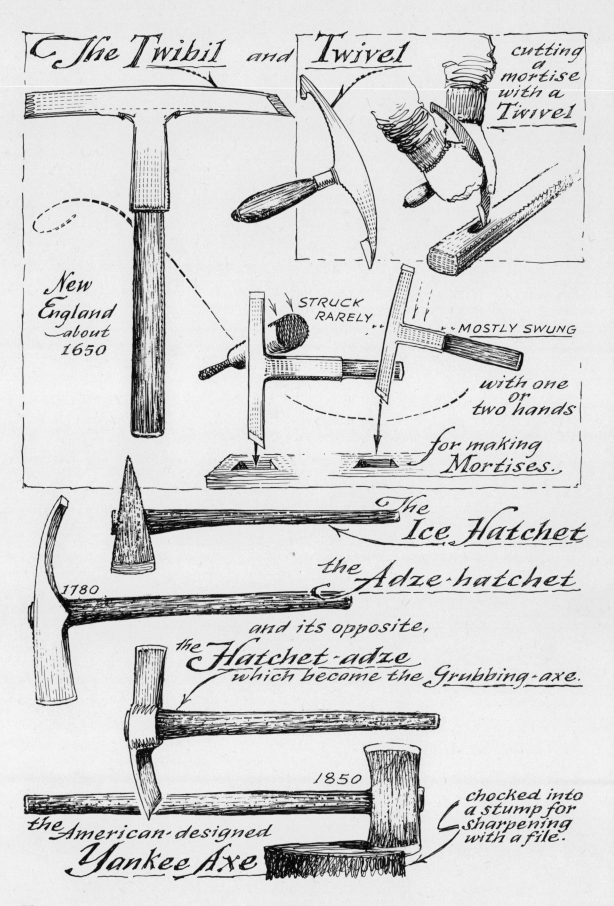

The Twibil and Twivel

cutting a mortise with a Twivel

New England about 1650

STRUCK RARELY

MOSTLY SWUNG

with one or two hands

for making Mortises.

The Ice Hatchet

the Adze-hatchet

1780

and its opposite, the Hatchet-adze which became the Grubbing-axe.

1850

chocked into a stump for sharpening with a file.

the American-designed Yankee Axe

The Chisel

There are so many kinds of chisels that it is difficult to establish definite nomenclature; yet, on the opposite page, we have attempted a general classification. The firmer (or firming or forming) chisel is the basic chisel design; it did a great many jobs, but one special use was to cut the superfluous wood from two auger holes to make a mortise. The framing chisel is a heavier version, and it was used largely in the cutting of tenons to fit the mortises. Both of these tools are wood-handled (usually socketed) and were designed to be struck with a mallet. The socket-end can be struck bare, without the handle, though a good craftsman seldom did this.

The short, stout mortise chisel is almost square, a one-purpose tool. The giant paring chisel, known as a slick, has a big blade that curves very slightly toward the bevel; it was designed, not for striking, but to be used with two hands (often with some shoulder help) like a giant plane. Big framing chisels are often misnamed slicks; if the curve is evident, it is a slick; if not, it is a giant framing chisel.

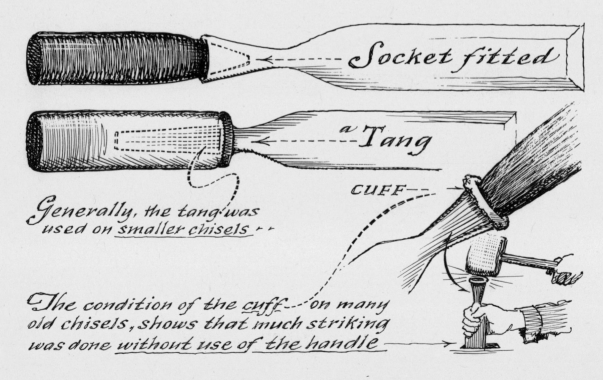

Socket fitted

a Tang

CUFF

Generally, the tang was used on *smaller chisels*

The condition of the *cuff* on many old chisels, shows that much striking was done *without use of the handle*

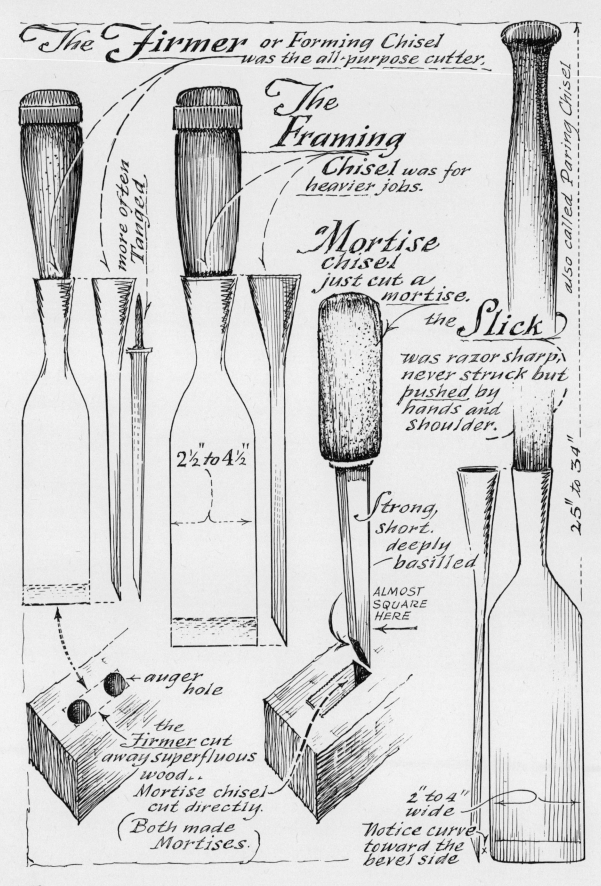

The *Firmer* or Forming Chisel was the all-purpose cutter.

The **Framing**
Chisel was for heavier jobs.

"Mortise chisel just cut a mortise.

the *Slick*

was razor sharp, never struck but pushed by hands and shoulder.

more often Tanged

2½" to 4½"

Strong, short, deeply basilled

ALMOST SQUARE HERE

also called Paring Chisel

25" to 34"

auger hole

the *Firmer* cut away superfluous wood..
Mortise chisel cut directly.
(Both made Mortises.)

2" to 4" wide
Notice curve toward the bevel side

Chisels and Gouges

What many call a "round chisel" is really a "gouge." The story told on the opposite page is that the earliest gouges were usually all metal (blacksmith-made from the Old World) and copied in this country in larger form for use with wooden handles.

The 1775 gouge in the illustration has an interesting story. It was found in a stone fence. Bright and silverish, its edge is keen; it has no rust. How farm-bound bog iron, privately smelted, hammered together at a farm forge, could be better in any way than today's steel is a mystery. I have compared the best chisels (the most expensive, that is) by leaving them in the rain alongside this ancient tool. The new tool's edge was dulled, and rust appeared within a few days.

The legend is that early surface ore contained much manganese and was purer in iron content. It is also believed that the use of charcoal gave purer carbon content and made a superior iron.

The chisels shown below had individual uses; some were used as bark scrapers, others as beam smoothers (like big planes). But I cannot find them listed or catalogued. Some ice chisels are similar, but they lack a tilted bit (see below—x).

x

this one was used in a clapboard mill.

all iron

5″

wood

Specially made Chisels of the 1800's

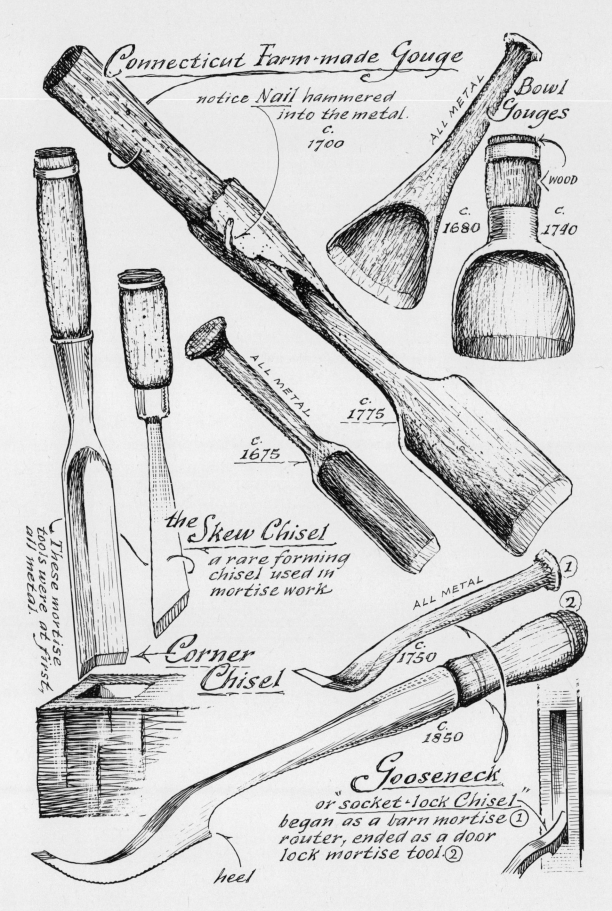

Connecticut Farm-made Gouge

notice Nail hammered into the metal. c. 1700

Bowl Gouges

ALL METAL

c. 1680

WOOD

c. 1740

ALL METAL

c. 1775

c. 1675

These mortise tools were at first, all metal.

the Skew Chisel

a rare forming chisel used in mortise work

← Corner Chisel

ALL METAL

c. 1750

①

②

c. 1850

Gooseneck

or "socket-lock Chisel" began as a barn mortise ① router, ended as a door lock mortise tool. ②

heel

55

Planes

Old World planes, made as much to look at as to do a job, often had inscriptions and floral carving. But the completely utilitarian American plane, except for an occasional graceful handle, usually resembled a box. Looking alike, a nest of small planes in the average carpenter's chest often reached thirty or more. Perhaps because of their plainness, or their quantity, they never caught the collector's fancy. Not long ago in Vermont, you could buy them by the barrel as firewood for five dollars. That included the barrel!

From the big ones ("long" planes) down, these either leveled the surface or fit pieces (side by side) together. Leveling was called "trying" and "trueing"; fitting was called "jointing."

With the trying plane (top, opposite) was a smaller bench plane called a jack plane and a larger (now rare) mate, the long jointer, or floor plane. But all other planes bow to their granddaddy in size, the cooper's long jointer, which was used upside down on a pair of legs to work the piece. Restricted in use mostly to joining barrel staves, this plane sometimes had two blades—one for rough, one for fine cut.

a Favorite Hand-made Plane

Natural Handle of oak

bit or "Iron" made from an old file.

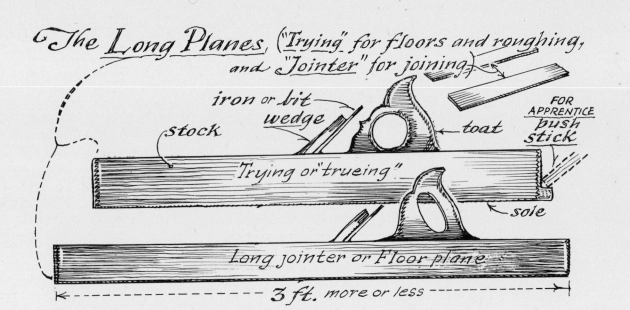

The *Long Planes*, ("Trying" for floors and roughing, and "Jointer" for joining)

iron or bit wedge

stock

toat

FOR APPRENTICE push stick

Trying or "trueing"

sole

Long jointer or Floor plane

3 ft. more or less

the *Cooper's Long Jointer* was used "upside down."

1600's

STAVE

1700's

. . nearly 6 ft. long!

Here are some general dimensions

Names of Planes	length	width	iron width
Modelling Plane	1" to 5"	¼" to 2"	3/16" to 1½"
Smoothing Plane	6" to 8"	2½" to 3½"	1¾" to 2 3/8"
Rabbet Plane	9½"	3/8" to 2"	3/8" to 2"
Jack Plane	12" to 17"	2½" to 3"	2" to 2¼"
Long or Trying Plane	20" to 26"	3½"	2½" to 2 5/8"
Jointer Plane or Floor Plane	28" to 36"	3¾"	2¾"
Cooper's long jointer	60" to 72"	5" to 5½"	3½" to 3¾"

The Moulding Plane

The grandest plane was the crown moulding plane. That large strip between the wall and ceiling was the identification of a fine room as well as the mark of the craftsman. No workman even carried about so large a tool and few owned one; instead the ordinary workman improvised with the basic "hollow" and "round" planes to make a moulding that the crown could do at one sweep.

The big crown plane was so heavy that it had bars for the apprentice to pull it by rope (1). Or, looped once or twice around a mill-wheel shaft (2), it could be pulled by tightening the rope, released by loosening.

Some crown planes had an apprentice pulling stick (3); others had a bar screwed across the front of the stock (4); others had two bars that slid into the front and back of the stock (5), with a notch for a second apprentice to push by stick.

The simplest moulding plane made a bead, but even this design came in sets of eight (from an eighth of an inch to a full inch), so you can see how a well-equipped carpenter's chest often had twenty or more moulding planes.

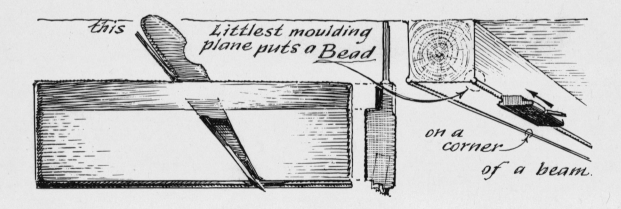

this   Littlest moulding
plane puts a Bead

on a
corner
of a beam.

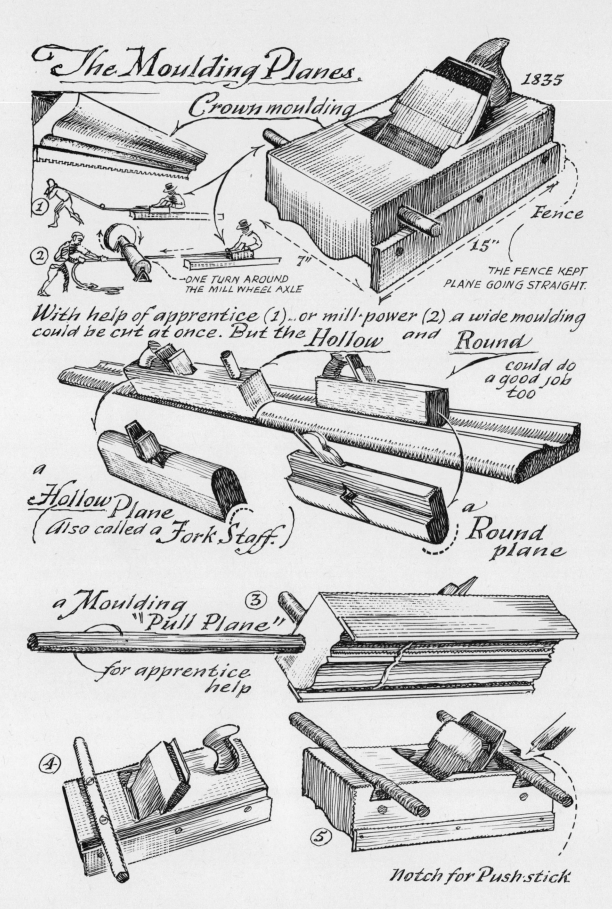

"The Moulding Planes

Crown moulding

1835

① ②

ONE TURN AROUND
THE MILL WHEEL AXLE

7"

Fence

15"

THE FENCE KEPT
PLANE GOING STRAIGHT.

With help of apprentice (1)...or mill-power (2) a wide moulding
could be cut at once. But the **Hollow** and **Round**

could do
a good job
too

a **Hollow** Plane
(Also called a Fork Staff.)

a **Round** plane

a Moulding
"Pull Plane" ③

for apprentice
help

④

⑤

Notch for Push-stick

The Rabbet

Most American carpenters call it a "rabbit"; the British call it a "rebate." It is really the "rabbet plane" that "rabbets" out a cut in the sides of boards, so that they may be overlapped and joined. This was the popular way of joining before milled tongue-and-groove.

The first rabbet and the long rabbet plane have fences (overlapping strips) to guide the plane along the end of the board (as shown on the opposite page). Because the little rabbet stands flat without a fence, it needs a strip of wood nailed along its route to guide it before it can properly cut a rabbet in a board.

These planes vary in design, some throwing shavings to the right, some to the left, some to both sides. Some irons have blades set, instead of at a right angle, on a skew to the stock to avoid tearing the wood. Rarer is the pistol-grip-handled rabbet, which lacks the usual wedge for holding the iron. Below is the rabbet saw, rarely used except in stairmaking.

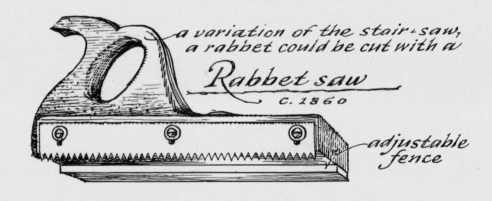

a variation of the stair-saw, a rabbet could be cut with a

Rabbet saw
C. 1860

adjustable fence

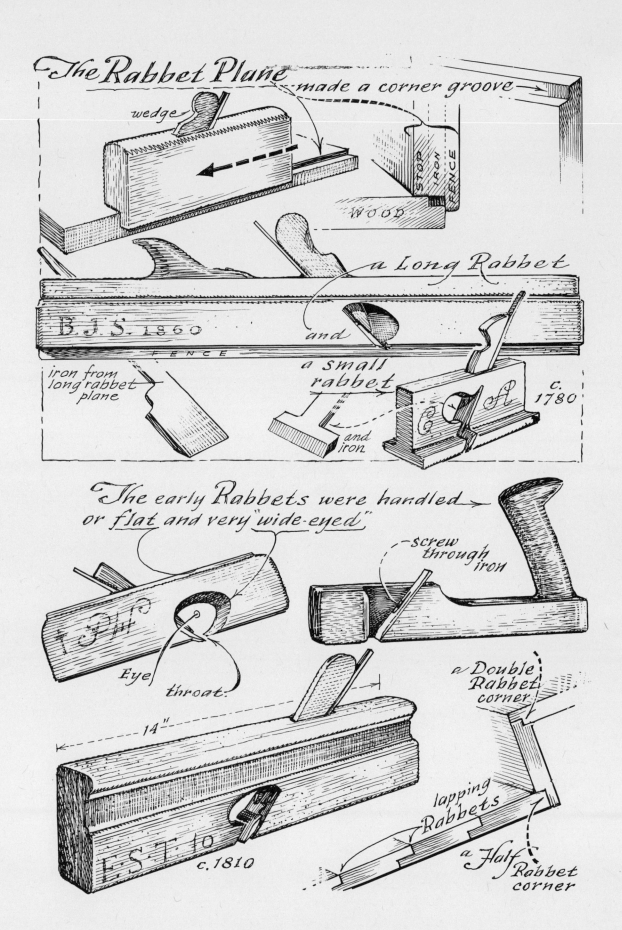

The Rabbet Plane — made a corner groove ⟶

wedge

STOP IRON
IRON
FENCE
WOOD

a Long Rabbet

B.J.S. 1860

FENCE

and

iron from long rabbet plane

a small rabbet

and iron

c. 1780

"The early Rabbets were handled ⟶ or flat and very "wide-eyed""

screw through iron

Eye

throat

14"

a Double Rabbet corner

E.S.T. 10   c. 1810

lapping Rabbets

a Half Rabbet corner

The Plow

The plow plane did the simplest job, yet it looks like the most complicated of tools. It just makes a groove. We use tongue-and-groove cuts for flooring and sheathing without realizing how recent this practice is. Before the "tongue" was popular, two grooves were placed against each other, and a "spline" was driven into the "tunnel" to join the two pieces together. For paneling, a tongue was not planed, but a "feather edge" was set into the groove.

The adjustable plow had its fence attached to the plane by two arms that slid through the plane stock and made secure by wooden wedges. Later the square arms became two long round screws with threaded knobs to hold them secure.

The unadjustable plow and unadjustable tongue plane came in pairs ("tongue-and-groove sets"), and there was also a combination of the two, set into one stock (see following pages).

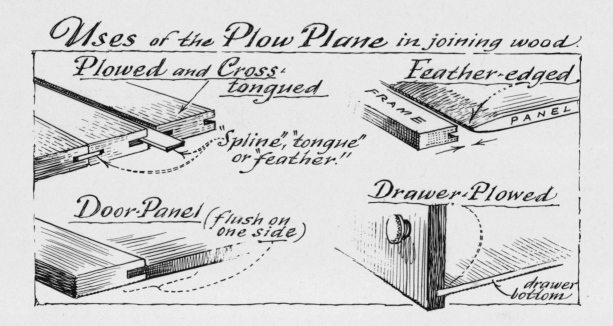

Uses of the Plow Plane in joining wood.

Plowed and Cross-tongued

Feather-edged

FRAME PANEL

"Spline", "tongue" or "feather."

Door-Panel (flush on one side)

Drawer-Plowed

drawer bottom

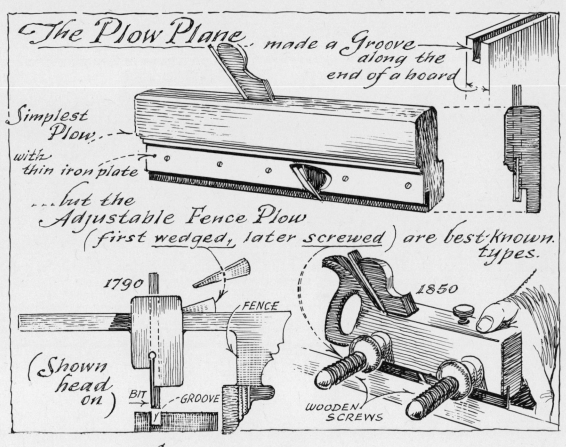

The Plow Plane ... made a Groove along the end of a board

Simplest Plow with thin iron plate

...but the *Adjustable Fence Plow* (first wedged, later screwed) are best-known types.

1790

FENCE

(Shown head on)

BIT — GROOVE

1850

WOODEN SCREWS

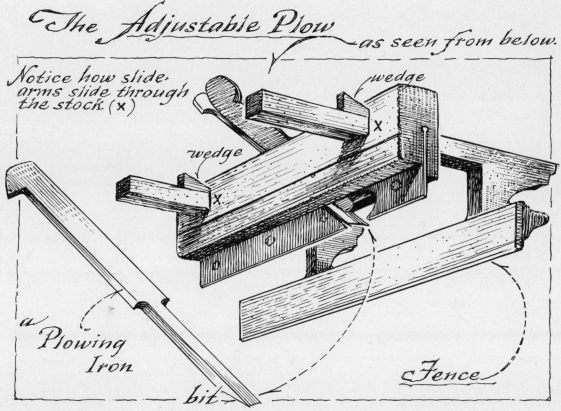

The Adjustable Plow as seen from below.

Notice how slide arms slide through the stock (x)

wedge

X

wedge

X

a Plowing Iron

bit

Fence

PLANES,

FOR

CARPENTERS, COOPERS, CABINET AND COACH MAKERS.

	Cast Steel. Single.	Cast Steel. Double.	German Steel. Single.	German Steel. Double.
Jointers 30 inch	$1 70	$2 17	$1 58	$2 05
do 28 "	1 64	2 08	1 52	1 96
do 26 "	1 58	2 00	1 46	1 88
do 22 "	1 50	1 92	1 38	1 80
do 21 "	1 42	1 84	1 30	1 72
Jack Planes	96	1 37½	88	1 30
Smooth Planes	87½	1 25	80	1 17
do Circular	92	1 31	84	1 23

	Cast Steel. Single.	Cast Steel. Double.	German Steel. Single.	German Steel. Double.
Cooper's Jointers	$2 50	$3 50	$2 88	$3 88
do stock howel	2 50	pl'd 3 00	2 38	2 88
do circ. leveler	1 50	" 2 00	1 38	1 87
do with handles	2 00	2 50	1 88	2 38
do crows	2 50			
Tooth Planes	1 25			
Miter Planes	1 00			

Ogees for Cabinet Makers, $1 00 per inch.

Astragals ¼ to ½ inch	62½
do ⅝ to 1 inch	75
Beads ⅛ to ¾ inch	75
do over 1 inch	87½
do full boxed ⅛ to ⅜	92
do do ½ to ¾	1 00
Coves to ¾ inch	62½
do ⅞ to 1 inch	75
Cove and Beads ⅜ to ½ inch	75
do do ⅝ to 1 inch	87½
do do over 1 inch	1 00
Center Beads to ⅜	87
Dadoes, slide stop	1 37
do screw stop	2 00
Fillisters	1 50
do with stop	1 75
do do and cut	2 00
do do cut and boxed	2 25
do with screw stop, cut and boxed	3 00
Guages	20
do oval head	25
Gothic Beads	1 25
Grecian Ovolos ⅜ by ¾ inch	1 00
do do ½ by 1 inch, ⅝ by 1¼	1 12½
do do ¾ by 1½ inch	1 25
do do Beads ⅜ by ⅞ in., ½ by 1⅛ in.	1 25
do do do ⅝ by 1⅜.—¾ by 1½ in.	1 50
do do do ⅞ by 1¾ and 2 inch	1 75
do Ogee and Bevel sq. ⅜ by ⅞ in. ½ by 1⅛ in.	1 25
do do do ⅝ by 1⅜ in. ¾ by 1½ in.	1 50
do do do ⅞ by 1¾ and 2 inch	1 75
Halving planes	62½
do do plated	87½
do do with handles	1 00
do do plated, with handles	1 25
Hollows and Rounds 9 pair to No. 18.	10 50
Match Planes for Boards ⅜ to 1 inch	1 75
do fence plated	2 00
do for Plank 1¼ inch	2 62½

Match Planes, fence plated	3 00
do moving fence	4 00
do screw arms	6 00
Plows, 1st rate, 8 irons	7 00
do 2d " "	6 00
do 3d " "	5 00
do 4th " "	4 50
Extra for boxing fence	50
Extra for side screws	50
do screw arms and 8 irons	7 00
do box fence	7 50
do side screws	8 00
do solid box	8 00
do do side screws	8 50
Rabbet Planes to 1 inch square 62, skew	75
do 1¼ inch 68, skew	87½
do 1½ inch 75, skew	92
do 1¾ inch 78, skew	1 00
do 2 inch	1 12½
do with handles	2 00
Extra for boxing	25
Extra for adding cut	25
Raising Planes, common	1 75
do moving fence	3 25
do do 3 in. iron	4 00
do do 3½ "	4 50
do do 4 "	5 00
Reeding Planes ⅛ to ½ inch	1 00
Sash Planes, 1 iron 1 00, boxed	1 50
do 2 " 1 50, "	2 00
do double 2 50, "	3 00
Snipe Bills	75
do full box	1 00
Side Rabbets	62½
Torus Beads to ¾ inch	75
do from ¾ to 1 inch	87½
do over 1 inch	1 00
Table Planes, pair	1 50
do boxed	2 00

Omitting various moulding planes and special planes (such as those illustrated on the opposite page), the above advertisement of the 1800's lists some of the basic planes that the average carpenter was likely to have in his chest. As many of these planes came in sets of eight, the army of old-time wooden planes seems overwhelming.

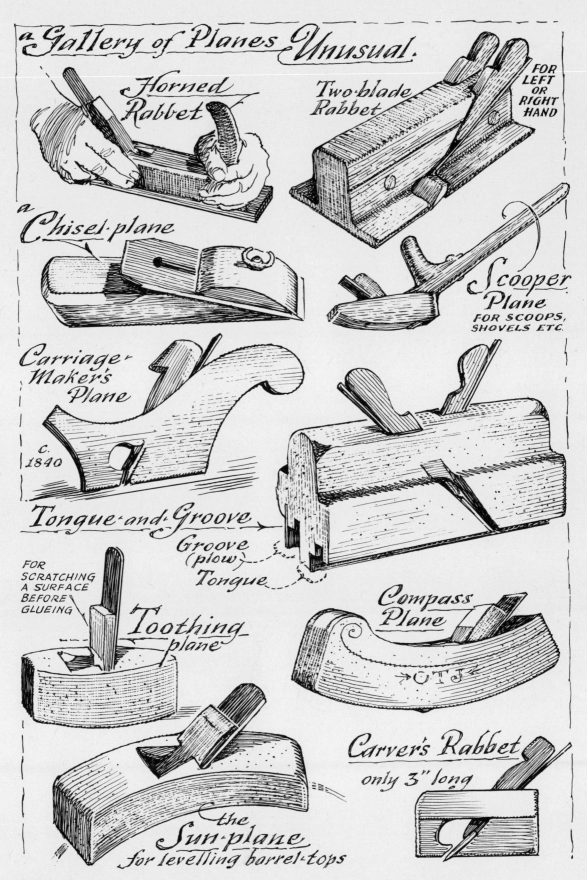

a Gallery of Planes Unusual.

Horned Rabbet

Two-blade Rabbet

FOR LEFT OR RIGHT HAND

a Chisel-plane

Scooper Plane

FOR SCOOPS, SHOVELS ETC.

Carriage-Maker's Plane

c. 1840

Tongue-and-Groove

Groove (plow)

Tongue

FOR SCRATCHING A SURFACE BEFORE GLUEING

Toothing plane

Compass Plane

← O T J →

Carver's Rabbet

only 3" long

the Sun-plane for levelling barrel-tops

Early American Saws

Both the frame saw and the open saw were in use during the first American settlements. The open saw is very much like its modern counterpart, but it had a handle like that of a knife and it was long enough to be used by two hands. Americans enjoyed using wood in their tools, and the wooden frame saw was most popular. Metal was hard to come by, and the frame saw had the advantage of needing only the narrowest blade.

Saw nomenclature is uncertain, but the most common division is that of "open" and "frame" types. The bow saw (again a frame type) was stretched taut between two arms by a twisted cord (or by rod and screw); the saw blade was readily turned by twisting the handles, making it easy to saw curved pieces.

The buck saw is a bow frame type, but its blade is stationary and heavier, and a long handle has been added. To "buck" logs was to saw them into proper lengths; hence, the buck saw is a woodsman's saw.

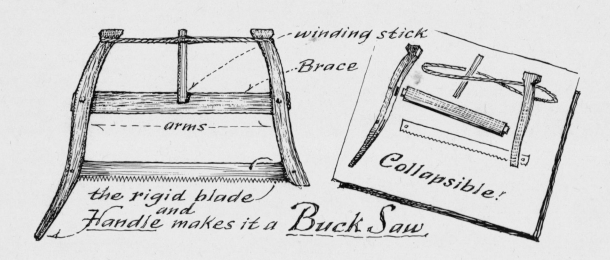

winding stick

Brace

arms

the rigid blade and Handle makes it a Buck Saw.

Collapsible!

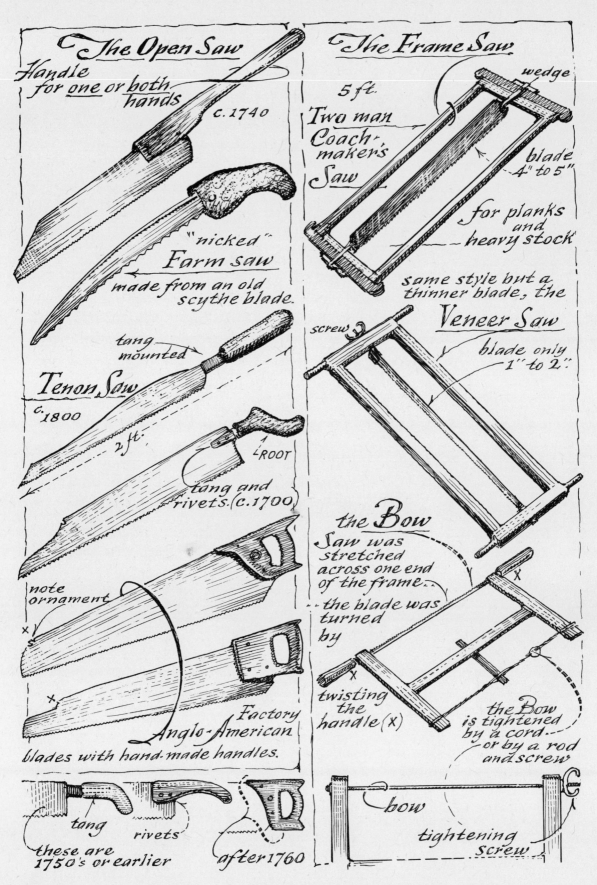

The Open Saw

Handle for one or both hands   c. 1740

"nicked" Farm saw
made from an old scythe blade.

tang mounted
Tenon Saw
c. 1800
2 ft.
ROOT
tang and rivets. (c. 1700)

note ornament
x
x

Factory Anglo-American
blades with hand-made handles.

tang   rivets
these are 1750's or earlier   after 1760

The Frame Saw

5 ft.
Two man Coach-maker's Saw   wedge

blade 4" to 5"

for planks and heavy stock

same style but a thinner blade, the
Veneer Saw
screw
blade only 1" to 2"

the Bow
Saw was stretched across one end of the frame...
the blade was turned by

x

x
twisting the handle (x)

the Bow is tightened by a cord... or by a rod and screw

bow
tightening screw

67

a Gallery of Frame Saws

The frame saw looks clumsy to us now, but actually it was much more of "an extension of the craftsman's hand" than the modern saw. You can cut straight or around corners with it and always see where the blade was cutting. The modern saw blade is wide, always covering the spot it is cutting, and is restricted to a straight cut.

The terms "chairmaker's saw," "felloe (also "felly") saw," "turning saw," etc. are difficult to pin to one model because each design overlapped the other in size or shape at one time or another. The frame saw is "strained" in the center and two stretchers keep it taut; the bow saw is strained on one end, with a stretcher cord (or rod) on the other.

The finer the work to be done the finer the saw; some frame saws are pieces of art both to work with and to look at.

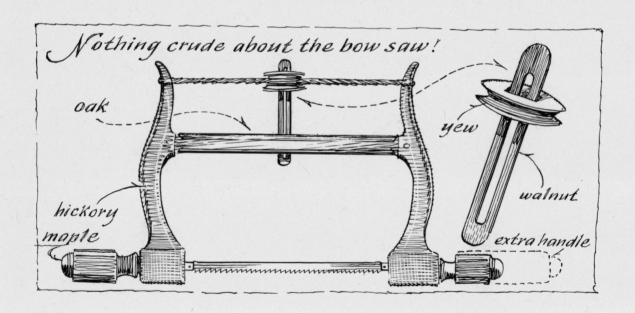

Nothing crude about the bow saw!

oak

yew

hickory maple

walnut

extra handle

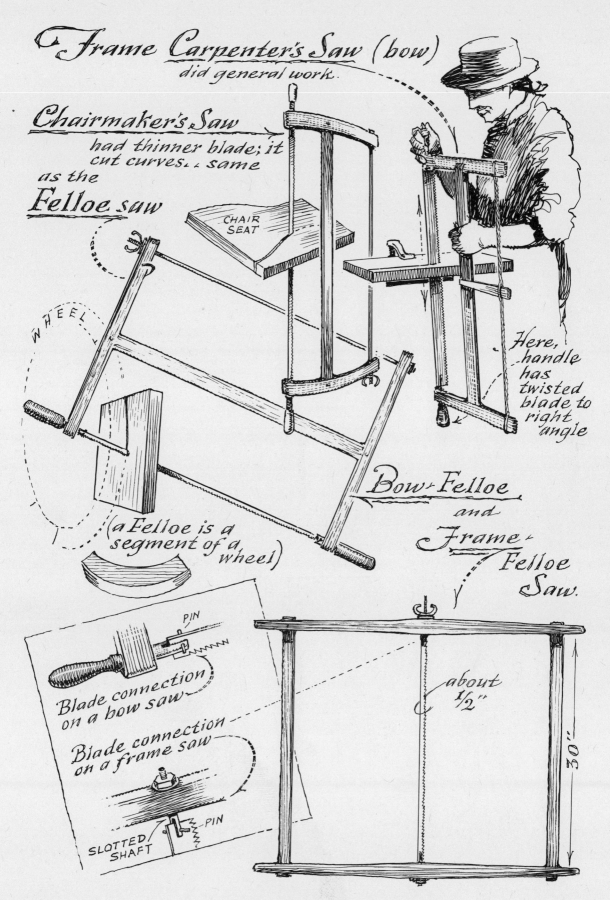

Frame Carpenter's Saw (bow)
did general work.

Chairmaker's Saw
had thinner blade; it cut curves.. same as the
Felloe saw

CHAIR SEAT

WHEEL

(a Felloe is a segment of a wheel)

Here, handle has twisted blade to right angle

Bow-Felloe
and
Frame-Felloe Saw.

PIN

Blade connection on a bow saw

Blade connection on a frame saw

SLOTTED SHAFT

PIN

about ½"

30"

The Biggest Saws

Its teeth raked to cut downward, the long pit saws (both open and framed) did most of the earliest American plank-sawing both from trestles and in pits. The open type was more recent in the New World than the framed model. Factory-made, the open pit saw was used until the late 1800's.

There was an ancient open plank saw (see below) that some collectors regard as an open pit saw, but the curved blade and matching handles indicate otherwise.

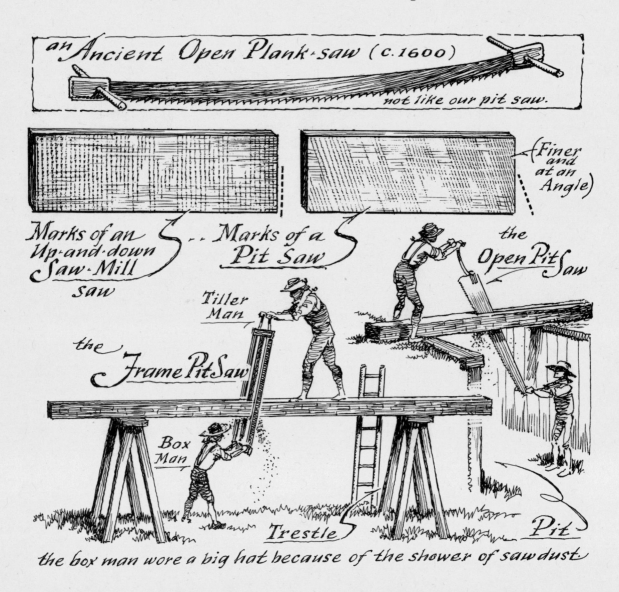

an Ancient Open Plank-saw (c. 1600)

not like our pit saw.

(Finer and at an Angle)

Marks of an Up-and-down Saw-Mill saw

Marks of a Pit Saw

the Open Pit Saw

Tiller Man

the Frame Pit Saw

Box Man

Trestle

Pit

the box man wore a big hat because of the shower of sawdust

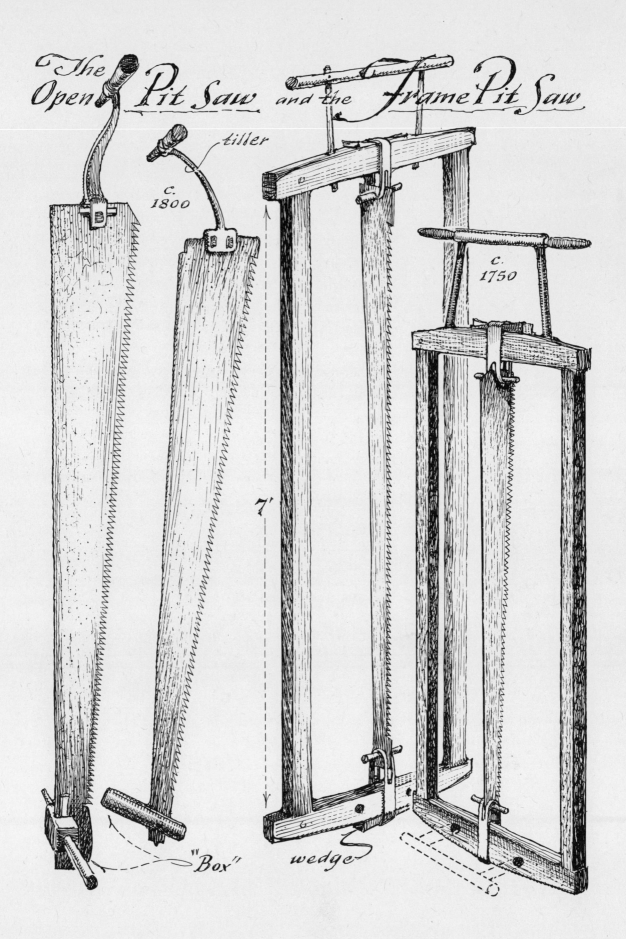

The Open *Pit Saw* and the *Frame Pit Saw*

tiller

c. 1800

c. 1750

7'

"Box"

wedge

71

to Make a Hole

Although awls seem no more than sharp points with handles, there are those who collect them as basic tools. The awl and punch enter wood by "spreading" the fibers apart; the ream, auger, and gimlet "cuts." The "burn auger" (1) was fired to a red-hot point that burned its opening in the wood; then it was twisted to make the hole deeper. The "wood punch" (2) was hammered into the wood, and was twisted both for deeper cut and for release. The "ream awl" (3) had sharp corners that acted as cutting agents.

The "gouge bit" (split-quill) was round-ended, like a gouging chisel; if water was put into its cavity it would run out the end. If water was dropped into a "spoon bit" or "pod auger," it would stay in, for the nose of the bit scoops upward into a twist (A and B). The "twisted cylinder" bit, neither podlike nor triangular, has parallel sides, one of which is a cutting edge. The cutter of the nose auger is shown below, along with the same device on a spiral-ribbon bit.

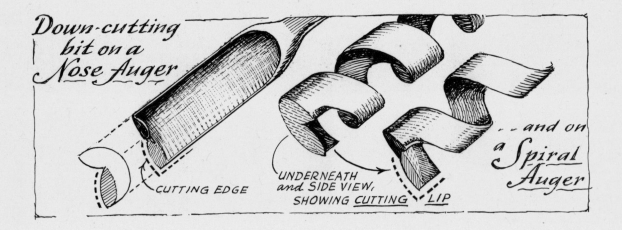

Down-cutting bit on a Nose Auger

CUTTING EDGE

UNDERNEATH and SIDE VIEW, SHOWING CUTTING LIP

...and on a Spiral Auger

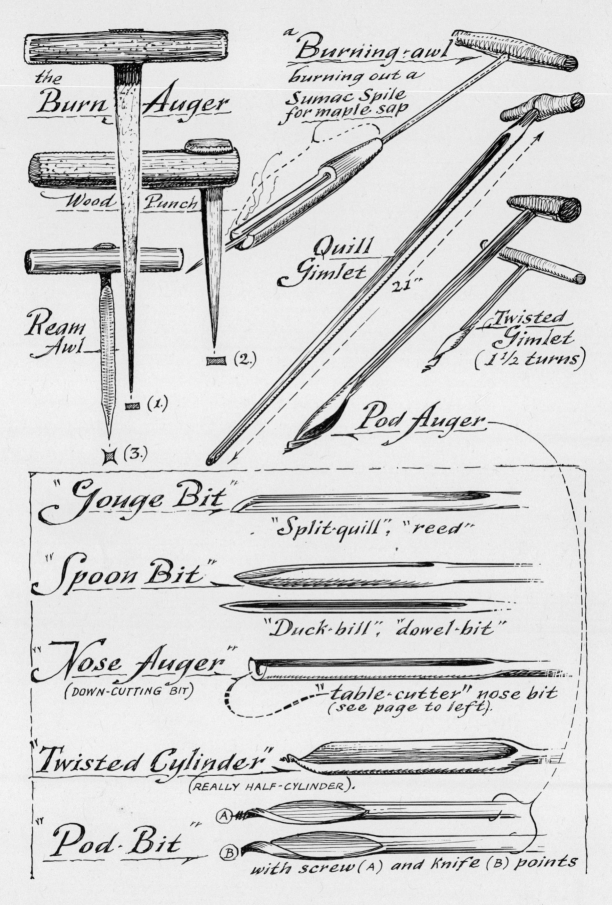

the
Burn Auger

Wood Punch

Ream Awl

(1.)
(2.)
(3.)

a Burning-awl
burning out a
Sumac Spile
for maple sap

Quill Gimlet

21"

Twisted Gimlet
(1½ turns)

Pod Auger

"Gouge Bit"
"Split-quill", "reed"

"Spoon Bit"
"Duck-bill", "dowel-bit"

"Nose Auger"
(DOWN-CUTTING BIT)
"table-cutter" nose bit
(see page to left).

"Twisted Cylinder"
(REALLY HALF-CYLINDER).

"Pod-Bit"
Ⓐ
Ⓑ
with screw (A) and knife (B) points

To Make a Hole Bigger

To enlarge a hole, you may "ream" it with a tapered blade; to be sure, the hole will be tapered too, but often (as when you are cutting a barrel bung-hole or a wheel hub-hole) this is just what you want. The biggest of all reamers is the wheelwright's hub reamer; often it reaches a length of three feet and weighs as much as twenty-five pounds. Some of these can still be found without handles and with strange hooks. Oddly enough, the experts have not decided just how these were used. But I rigged up a wagon wheel on a wheelwright's bench, then put a hooked reamer through the hub, which I had weighted with seventy-five pounds. With two men turning a very long detachable handle (which might explain the missing handles on so many of these blades it worked nicely). With an ordinary reamer, a man exerts about half his weight downward; this can be bettered with a seventy-five-pound weight plus the twenty-five-pound weight of the tool itself.

Tap augers and hub reamers were usually sharpened on one blade (on the inner side).

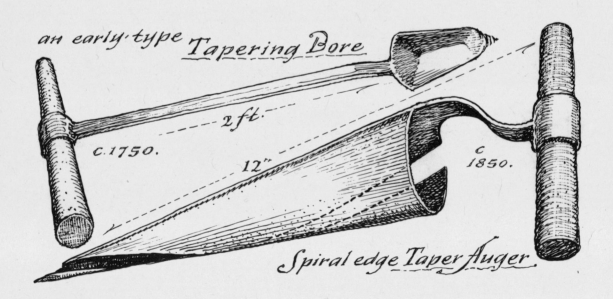

an early-type Tapering Bore

c. 1750.

2 ft.

12"

c 1850.

Spiral edge Taper Auger

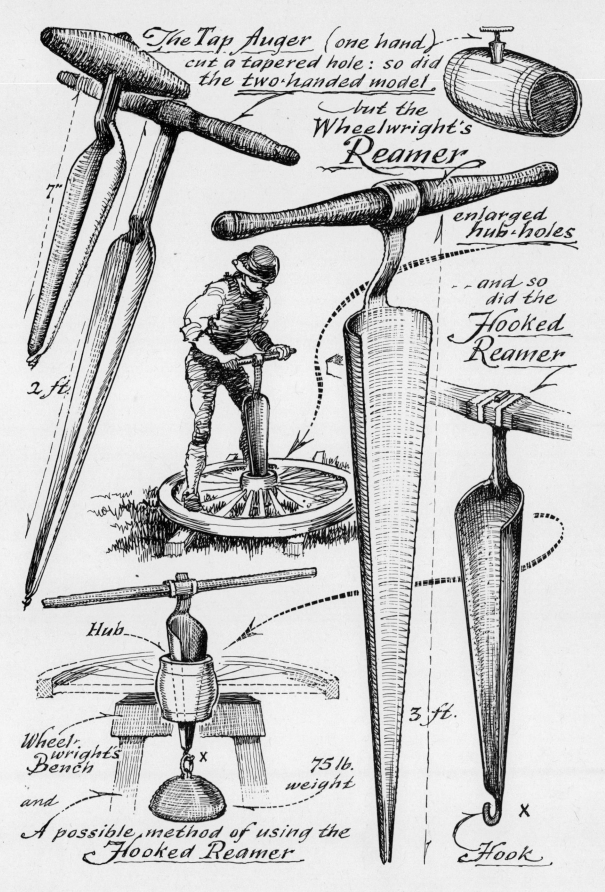

The Tap Auger (one hand)
cut a tapered hole: so did
the two-handed model

but the
Wheelwright's
Reamer

enlarged
hub-holes

...and so
did the
Hooked
Reamer

7"

2 ft.

Hub

3 ft.

Wheel-
wright's
Bench

and

75 lb.
weight

A possible method of using the
Hooked Reamer

Hook

X

X

75

to Make a Bigger Hole

Recently a "revolutionary speed bit" was introduced for electric drills. Actually it is an adaptation of an early "button bit" (A) and (B) and has the same design as the "center bit" (c. 1794) with which the pioneer American started trunnel holes in his buildings. For shallow holes or to start a boring, it cut downward without pulling shavings upward as the big spiral bit does. Center bits, therefore, which were never put on bar handles, were used with a brace.

The four typical wooden bar handles shown are generalizations; because so many men made their own handles, it is difficult to pinpoint the date of a handle from its design. I have worked out these estimates, from the handles in my own collection, in the hope that this information might be helpful in dating tools in other collections.

It seems incredible that a man could turn the huge bits that some augers have. The job was made easier in the 1800's by a two-handled drill (shown opposite); an adjustable model came out in the 1860's that drilled at any angle.

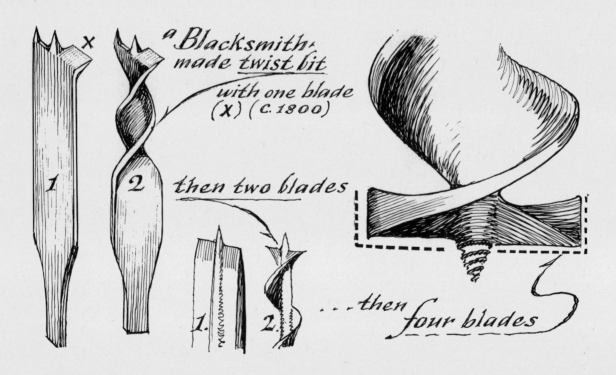

1

X

2

a *Blacksmith*-made *twist bit*
with one blade
(X) (c. 1800)

then two blades

1. 2.

...*then four blades*

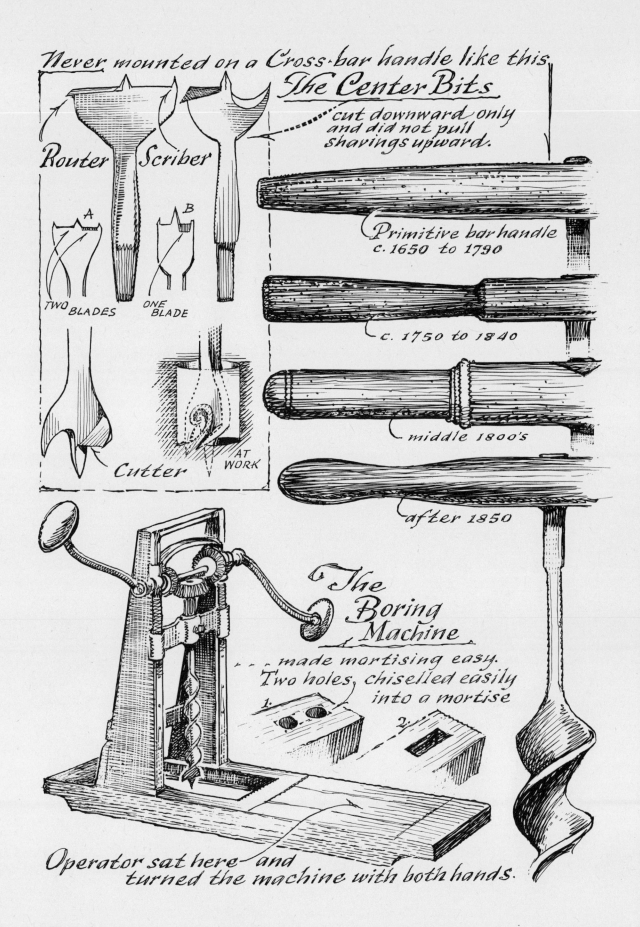

Never mounted on a Cross-bar handle like this.

The Center Bits

cut downward only and did not pull shavings upward.

Router   Scriber

A   B

TWO BLADES   ONE BLADE

Cutter   AT WORK

Primitive bar handle
c. 1650 to 1790

c. 1750 to 1840

middle 1800's

after 1850

The Boring Machine

--- made mortising easy.
Two holes chiselled easily into a mortise

1.   2.

Operator sat here and turned the machine with both hands.

The Brace or Bitstock

The early American bitstock or brace was made of native seasoned hardwood. Some of the earliest were made of natural-shaped roots or boughs (see drawing in center, opposite page). Oak and hickory were most commonly used although the burl-wood bitstock was also prized.

Most early braces (particularly in New England) were "bitted" in a permanent manner; the bit was moulded into a metal wad and fitted tightly into a square wooden chuck (sometimes ferruled), and this square chuck was wedged into the stock to stay.

The revolving buttons were masterpieces of woodworking, for most of those on the earliest braces still work nicely and are not even cracked. The button was either "stayed" by a wooden pin through the shaft and head (A), or the shaft was "stayed" by a "Cotter-pinlike" peg (B). The natural-shape stock's button was loose, staying in just by pressure. (As some braces were rested against the chest—and therefore needed a bigger and flatter button—this brace may have had interchangeable buttons, one for the hand and one for the chest.)

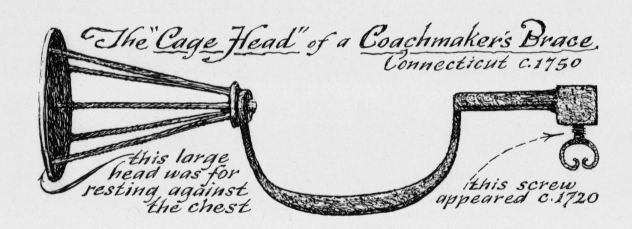

The "Cage Head" of a Coachmaker's Brace.
Connecticut c.1750

this large head was for resting against the chest

this screw appeared c.1720

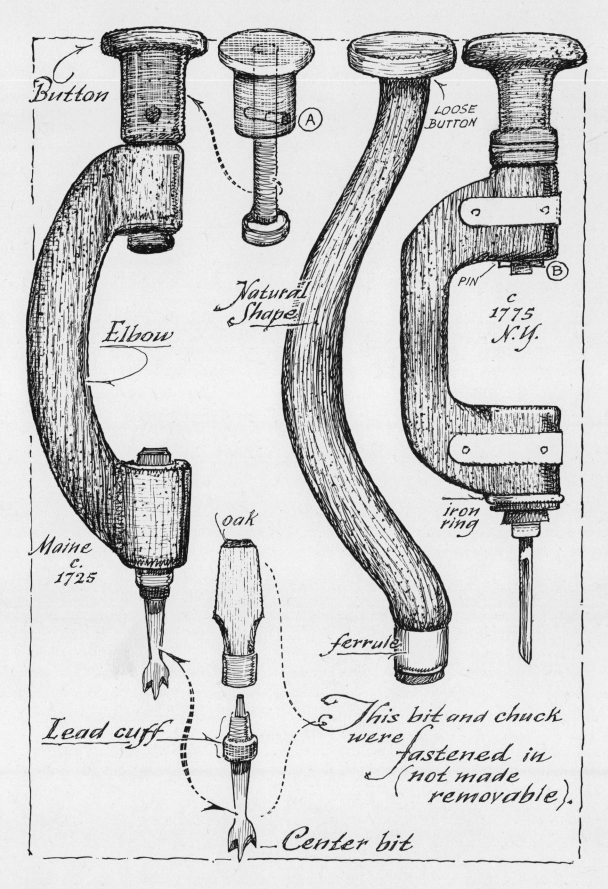

Button

Natural
Shape

A

Elbow

LOOSE
BUTTON

PIN

B

c
1775
N.Y.

Maine
c.
1725

oak

iron
ring

Lead cuff

ferrule

This bit and chuck
were fastened in
(not made
removable).

Center bit

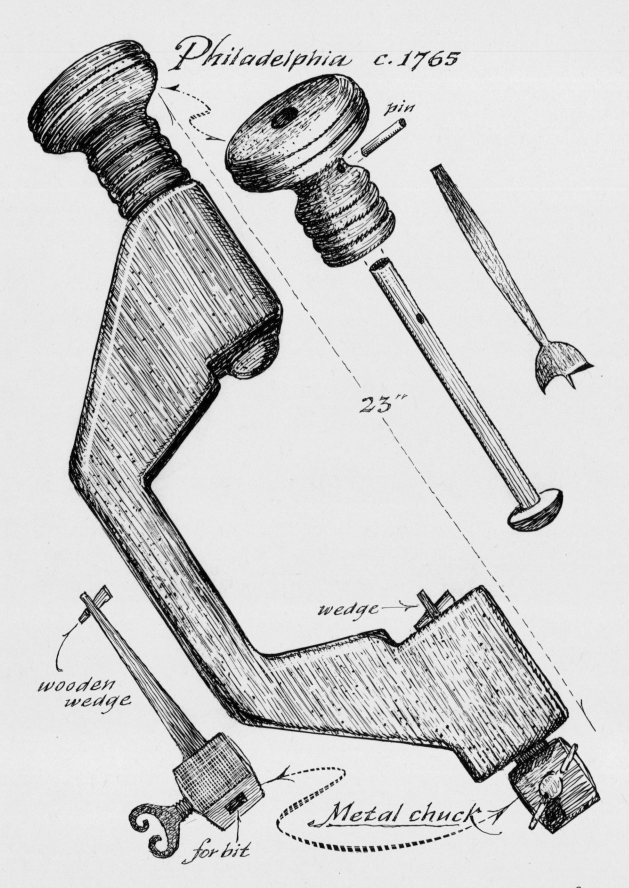

Philadelphia c.1765

pin

23"

wedge →

wooden
wedge

for bit

Metal chuck →

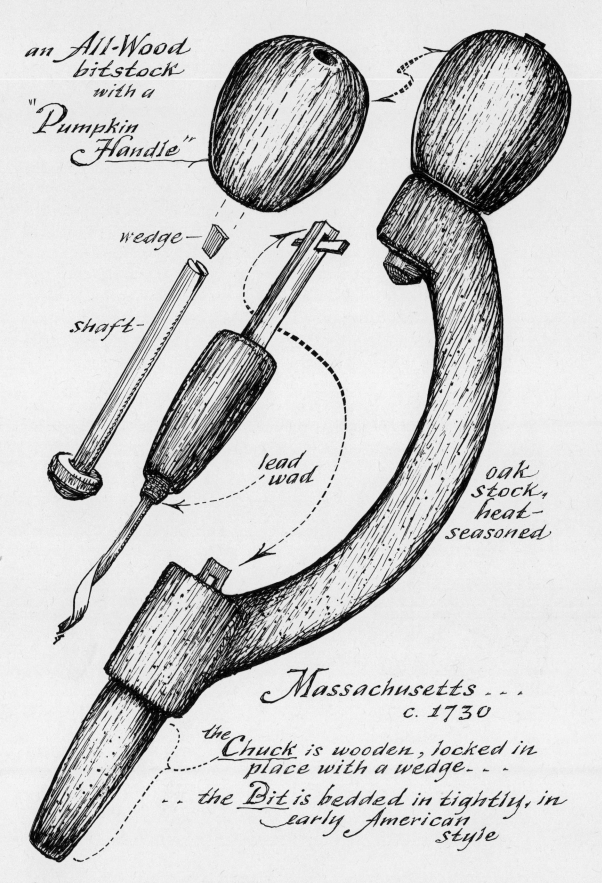

an All-Wood
bitstock
with a
"Pumpkin
Handle"

wedge—

shaft—

lead
wad

oak
stock,
heat-
seasoned

Massachusetts . . .
c. 1730

the *Chuck* is wooden, locked in
place with a wedge . . .
. . the *Bit* is bedded in tightly, in
early American
style

The THINGS you'll find in a Barn!

One of the most popular pages of the monthly publication of a tool collectors' club is its "Whatsis Column." Antique gadgets that stump the experts are frequently turning up. In the era of hand-made tools, it was logical that one-of-a-kind implements were created—the man who custom-made his own tools could allow himself the luxury of making tools to meet *his* needs. Then, too, there were devices that had many uses. Ladders were used as tobacco driers; the bars of a ladder-back chair held candleholders; meat hooks doubled as grappling hooks that retrieved things from the bottoms of wells. If you think it strange that a hook was so necessary to a household, remember that the well was used many times a day, that foods needing refrigeration were often lowered into it. Items lost beneath the water could not, of course, be seen, so they could be retrieved only by groping. The well hook was used as much as any other implement of the old-time household. After all, who wanted to drink water from a well filled with old pails?

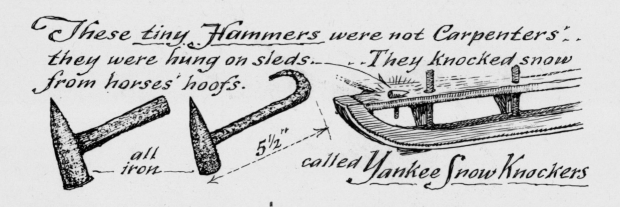

These tiny *Hammers* were not Carpenters'... they were hung on sleds...They knocked snow from horses' hoofs.

all iron

5½"

called Yankee Snow Knockers

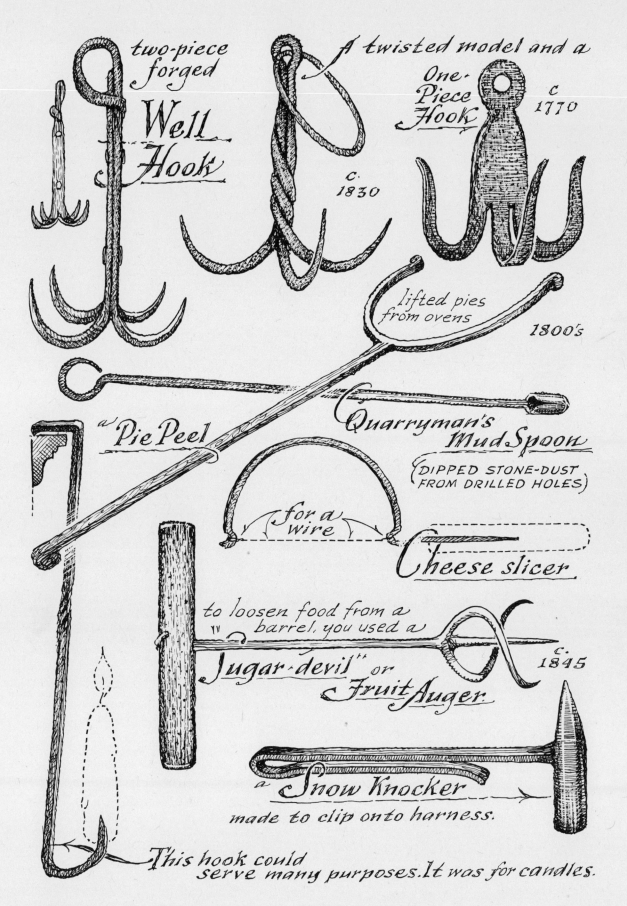

two-piece forged

Well Hook

A twisted model and a

One-Piece Hook
c. 1770

c. 1830

lifted pies from ovens
1800's

a **Pie Peel**

Quarryman's Mud Spoon
(DIPPED STONE-DUST FROM DRILLED HOLES)

for a wire

Cheese slicer

to loosen food from a barrel, you used a

Sugar-devil" or Fruit Auger.
c. 1845

a **Snow Knocker**
made to clip onto harness.

This hook could serve many purposes. It was for candles.

Some were Special

Although nails and hooks and tacks and hundreds of other iron implements were hammered out by farmers all over the countryside, it was recognized as fitting that each item have its own sizes and patterns. The nails made in Maine look quite like the nails made in New Jersey, both in proportions and design; only an expert can tell a difference. People were religious about conforming to tradition; they had a profound reverence for accepted design that we nowadays feel is decadence.

Here are a few things that are of the past that you might find in old attics or barns, each thing for a special use. The stock-knife shaped wood, the mill pick dressed millstones, the barrel-scrape cleaned out barrels, the "commander" pushed beams "home" and into their mortises.

When I was trying to move a barn, I found a "commander" of better use than two men working with sledgehammers, and was pleased to see it sending beams into place without disfiguring them as the iron sledges did.

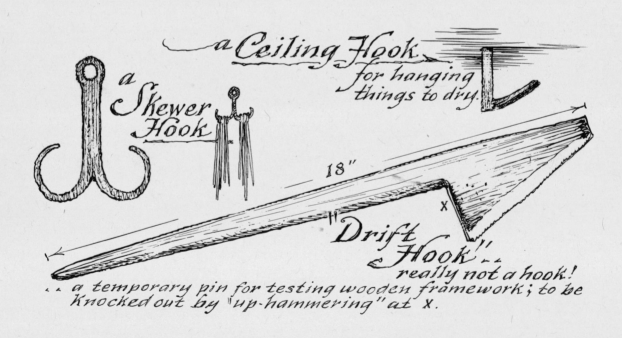

a Skewer Hook

a *Ceiling Hook* for hanging things to dry.

18"

Drift Hook.. really not a hook!

.. a temporary pin for testing wooden framework; to be knocked out by "up-hammering" at X.

The Stock-Knife.. also called Block-Knife

1815

fastened to a block, it cut out rough wood shapes for the woodworking shop

WOOD HANDLE

a stock-knife unearthed at Jamestown, Va.

The Mill Pick

another type

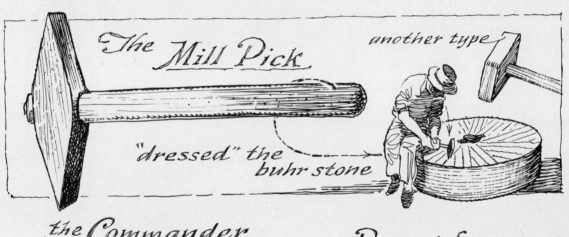

"dressed" the buhr stone

the Commander was swung between the legs..

MORTISE and TENON

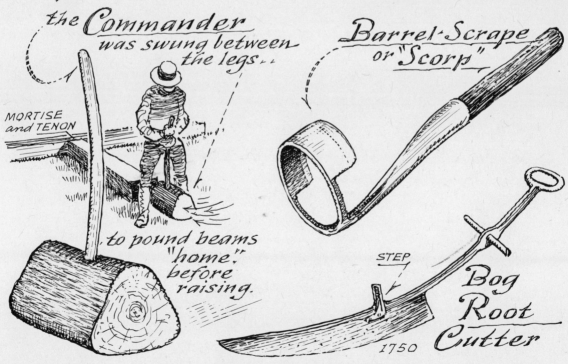

Barrel-Scrape or "Scorp"

to pound beams "home" before raising.

STEP

Bog Root Cutter

1750

85

These were Tools too!

"Sleds" were for winter; "sledges" were used year round. Tools the sledges were. If you would wish to learn the value of the sledge, try putting an ordinary house broom beneath a heavy trunk or object you wish to move. With someone then lifting one end, a child can easily pull the broom and its load across the floor. Farmers pulled unbelievable loads (on wooden runners) across grass on which a wheel would have sunk and become impossible. We know of the "stone boat," but the Early American farmer had a number of other sledge-type devices before the wheelbarrow. A sledge could be pulled by horse or ox through forest, and over rocks and onto the farm in winter ice or spring mud, whereas a wheeled vehicle could not. A wheeled vehicle is higher off the ground; this makes it inconveniently high for lifting loads *into* and it does tip over easily. So, harvesting and haying and moving rocks, dung, maple syrup barrels, etc. was done by sledge rather than wagon.

Here you may see a few of these early sliding devices. It might be safely said that for every wagon on the Early American farm, there were three to ten sledges. Even the hand-pulled model, like that shown below, was used until the early 1800's.

Even after horse and wagon vehicles, the *Tumbril Sledge* remained as a handy farm tool.

1650

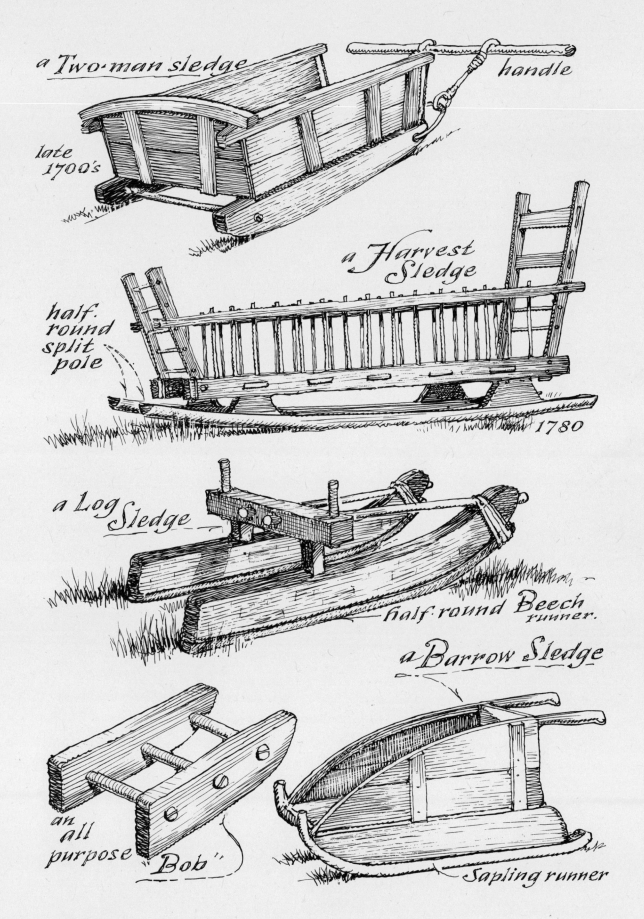

a Two·man sledge

handle

late 1700's

a Harvest Sledge

half-round split pole

1780

a Log Sledge

half·round Beech runner.

a Barrow Sledge

an all purpose "Bob"

Sapling runner

87

Jacks

The Early American was an artist at lifting and moving heavy objects. Foundations and stone fences were built with the lever principle and a few gadgets as well as with the help of oxen. Experts are often stumped by the strange hooks and loops of iron with teeth in them that are found in old barns. But these were blacksmith-made jack hooks for moving beams and logs and stones. The lever was any handy tree limb; the longer, the more leverage.

The "wagon jacks" you find in antique shops were used for many purposes. Carpenters, framers, blacksmiths, and wheelwrights included these jacks in their list of shop tools. Some of them are made entirely of wood (usually ash or hickory); and they have outlasted many automobile jacks that have rusted away and ended in the junk pile while the wooden jacks are as good as they were a century ago.

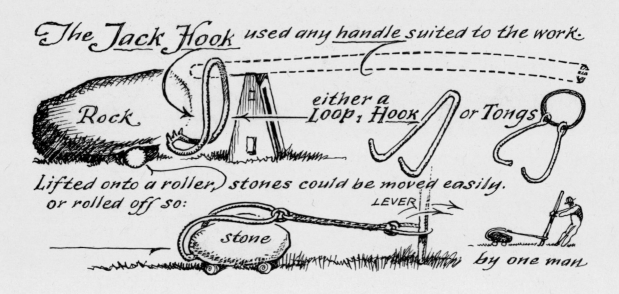

The Jack Hook used any handle suited to the work.

Rock — either a Loop, Hook or Tongs

Lifted onto a roller, stones could be moved easily. or rolled off so:

stone — LEVER — by one man

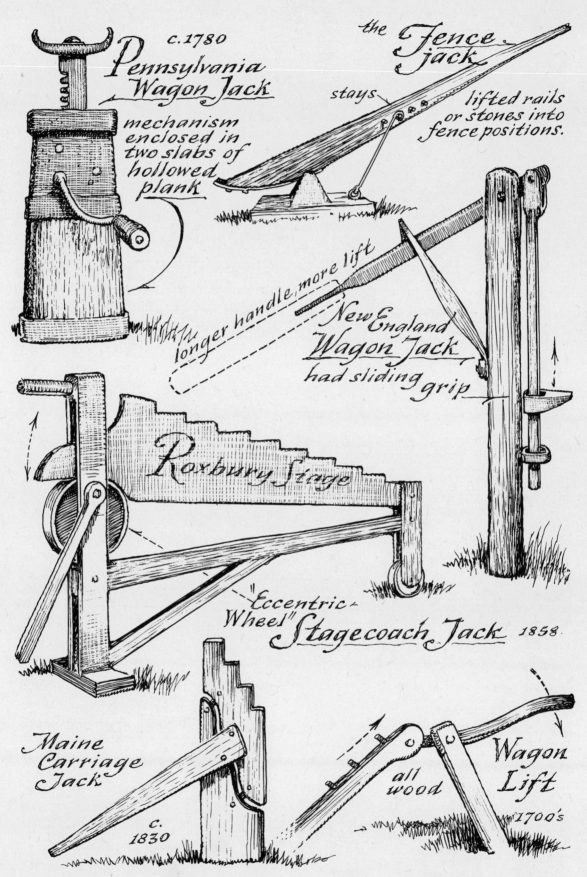

c. 1780

Pennsylvania Wagon Jack

the Fence Jack

mechanism enclosed in two slabs of hollowed plank

stays

lifted rails or stones into fence positions.

longer handle, more lift

New England Wagon Jack had sliding grip

Roxbury Stage

"Eccentric Wheel" Stagecoach Jack 1858.

Maine Carriage Jack

c. 1830

all wood

Wagon Lift

1700's

The Blacksmith

"Smith" from "smite," "black" from "black metal" (as distinguished from silversmith brightwork), the "blacksmith" was the Early American handyman. He made nails, hinges, sled runners, anchors, scythes, hoes, utensils, axes, hooks, and every kind of tool. In the middle 1800's he began taking over the farrier's work of horseshoeing; till then the farrier was veterinary too.

Blacksmith tool design has not changed very much except for the hazelwood withes that held all upper tools (chisels and swages). Hardly an implement or utensil cannot be traced to the early blacksmith.

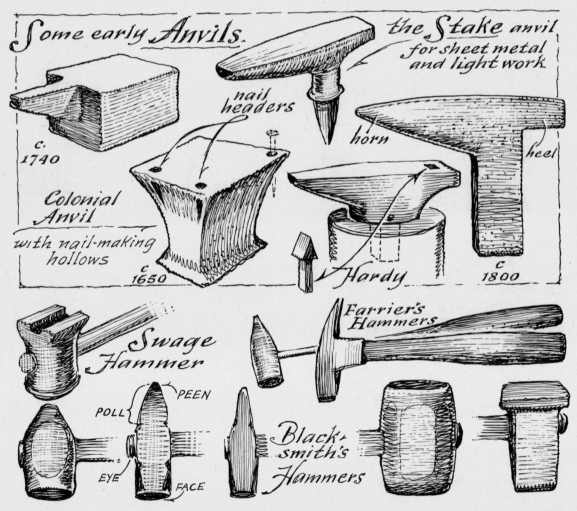

Some early Anvils.

the Stake anvil for sheet metal and light work

nail headers

horn

heel

c. 1740

Colonial Anvil

with nail-making hollows

c. 1650

Hardy

c. 1800

Swage Hammer

Farrier's Hammers

PEEN

POLL

EYE

FACE

Black-smith's Hammers

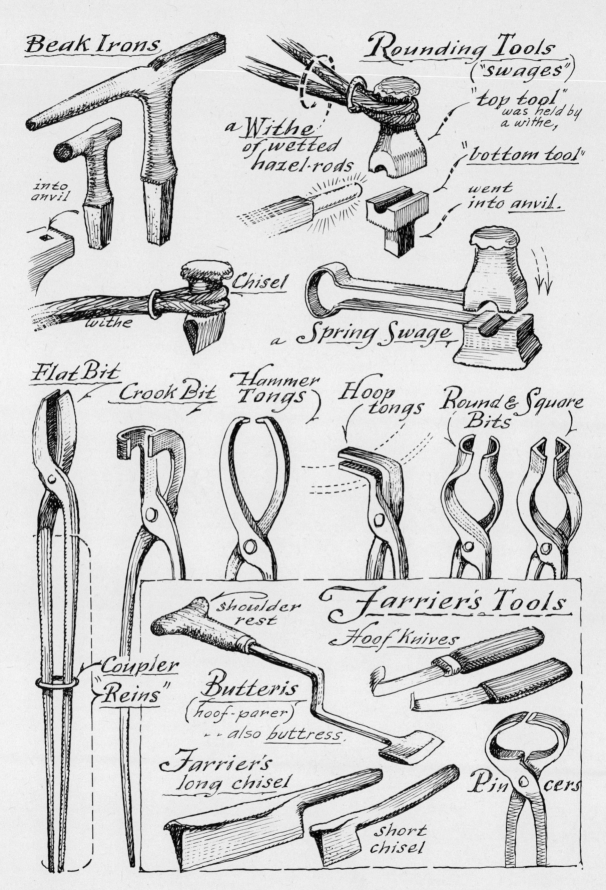

Beak Irons

into anvil

Rounding Tools ("swages")

a Withe of wetted hazel-rods

"top tool" was held by a withe,

"bottom tool" went into anvil.

Chisel

withe

a Spring Swage

Flat Bit   Crook Bit   Hammer Tongs   Hoop tongs   Round & Square Bits

"Coupler Reins"

shoulder rest   Farrier's Tools

Hoof Knives

Butteris (hoof-parer) -- also buttress.

Farrier's long chisel

short chisel

Pincers

Wrought Nailmaking

MACHINE-CUT   WROUGHT

Lacking in beauty, the "nail header" is hardly a collector's prize, yet its plainness does not adequately explain its infrequent appearance in antique shops. Considering how farmers made nails by the thousands during winter months around the forge or fireplace, the rarity of headers is a mystery.

Machine-cut nails taper only on two sides; wrought nails on four. The most common "rose nail" had four hammer hits (if done by an expert); the head of the "clasp nail" had sharp downward sides to cut into the surface; "plancher nails" had T-shaped heads to hold down flooring; the "scupper" nailed leather (as for a bellows). Though our "brad" is a small-headed nail, the word once meant "broad" and the "brad" was such a nail for planks.

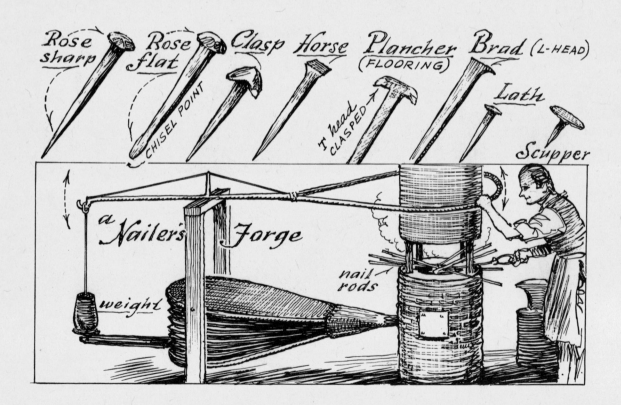

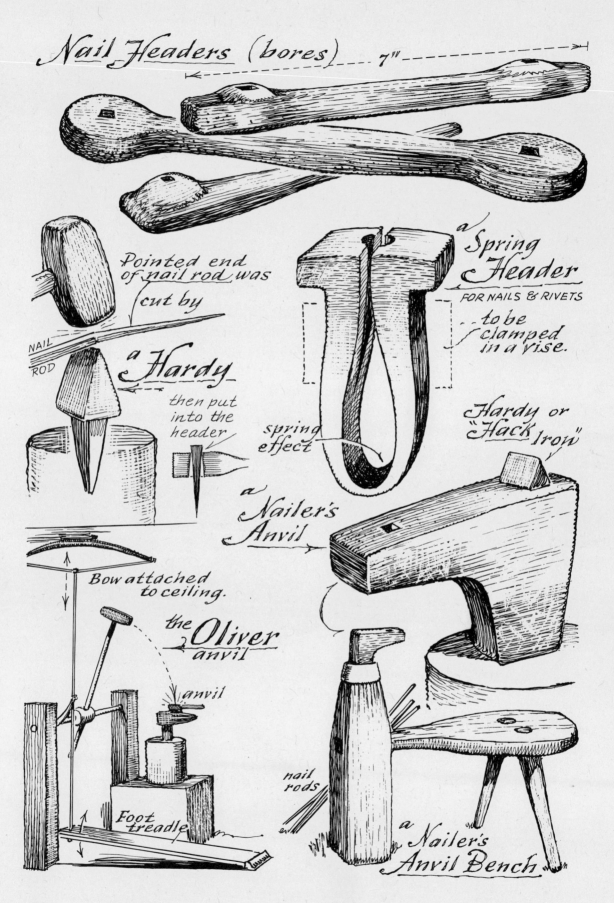

Nail Headers (bores) ---- 7" ----

Pointed end of nail rod was cut by

NAIL ROD

"a Hardy"

then put into the header

a Spring Header

FOR NAILS & RIVETS

to be clamped in a vise.

spring effect

a Nailer's Anvil

Hardy or "Hack Iron"

Bow attached to ceiling.

the Oliver anvil

anvil

Foot treadle

nail rods

a Nailer's Anvil Bench

Tanners and Curriers

A currier did *not* curry horses. His craft was to scrape and soften the rough hides after the tanner had treated them. The tanner's tools, so wet and messy when being used, were seldom things of beauty, but their lines were traditional and graceful. The tanner's knives had delicate curves to fit the curve of the tanner's beam.

The currier's beam was flat, just as his knife was. The shaving knife (also called beamer or head-knife) had a soft steel blade with its fine edge burred over (recurved) into a minute scraper form. This delicate edge needed constant turning with a "turning steel" and lifting with a "finger steel," which was kept handy between two fingers as the beamsman worked. (This recurved edge will have disappeared from wear and corrosion on ancient tools.)

Farmers made their own leather for shoes, hinges, and harness, so old barns often have such tools about.

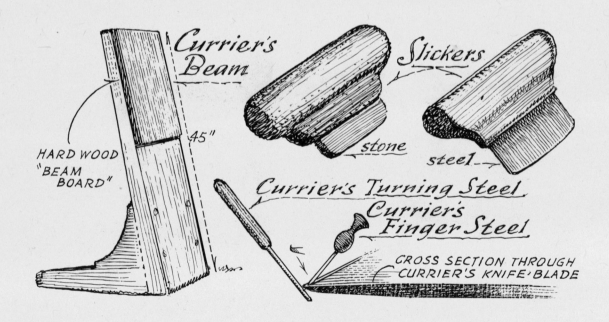

Currier's Beam

HARD WOOD "BEAM BOARD"

45"

Slickers

stone

steel

Currier's Turning Steel

Currier's Finger Steel

CROSS SECTION THROUGH CURRIER'S KNIFE BLADE

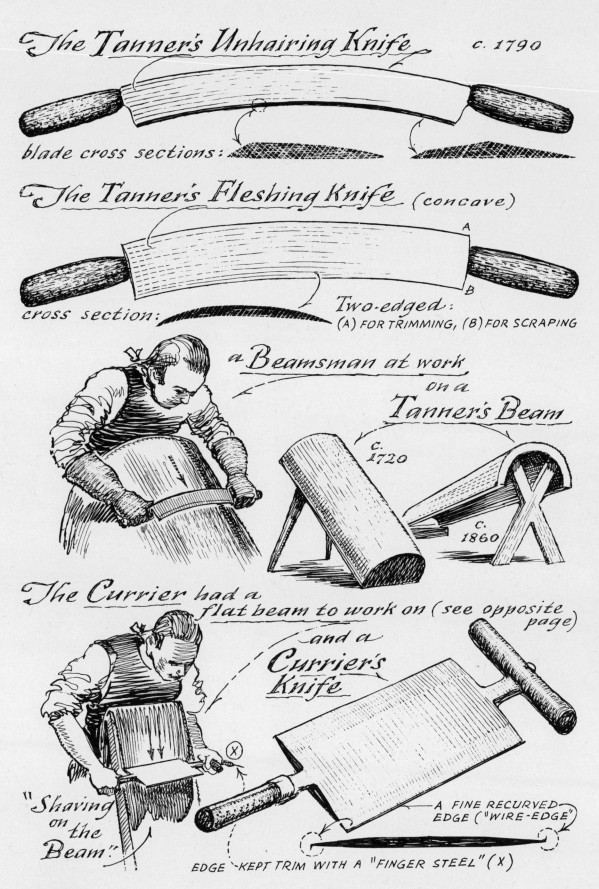

The Tanner's Unhairing Knife   c. 1790

blade cross sections:

The Tanner's Fleshing Knife (concave)

cross section: Two-edged:
(A) FOR TRIMMING, (B) FOR SCRAPING

a Beamsman at work on a Tanner's Beam

c. 1720

c. 1860

The Currier had a flat beam to work on (see opposite page)

and a *Currier's Knife*

"Shaving on the Beam"

A FINE RECURVED EDGE ("WIRE-EDGE")

EDGE KEPT TRIM WITH A "FINGER STEEL" (X)

About Wheels

Early wheelwright tools were not much different from those of hardwood joinery except for those shown here. The process of putting a wheel together is illustrated below. The tire (iron outer rim) was made by the blacksmith. After the tire was made hot in a bed of ashes, it was applied to the wooden wheel, and then cooled quickly. The contraction tightened the tire, and held the whole wheel together with a tremendous force.

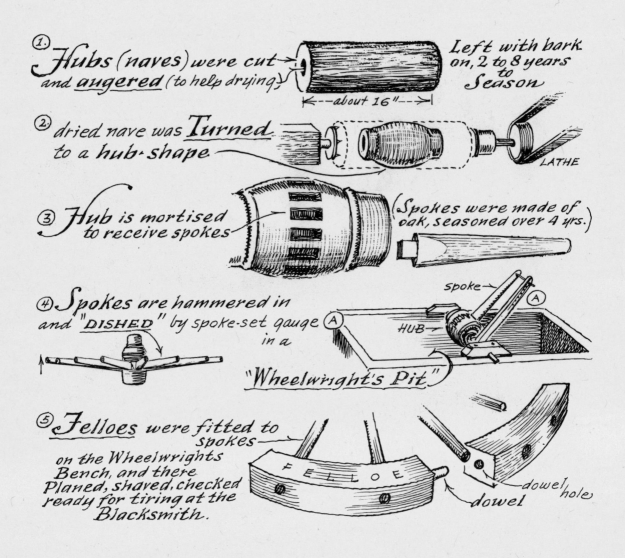

① Hubs (naves) were cut and augered (to help drying). Left with bark on, 2 to 8 years to Season
about 16"

② dried nave was Turned to a hub-shape. LATHE

③ Hub is mortised to receive spokes (Spokes were made of oak, seasoned over 4 yrs.)

④ Spokes are hammered in and "DISHED" by spoke-set gauge Ⓐ in a "Wheelwright's Pit" spoke→ Ⓐ HUB

⑤ Felloes were fitted to spokes on the Wheelwrights Bench, and there Planed, shaved, checked ready for tiring at the Blacksmith. FELLOE dowel dowel hole

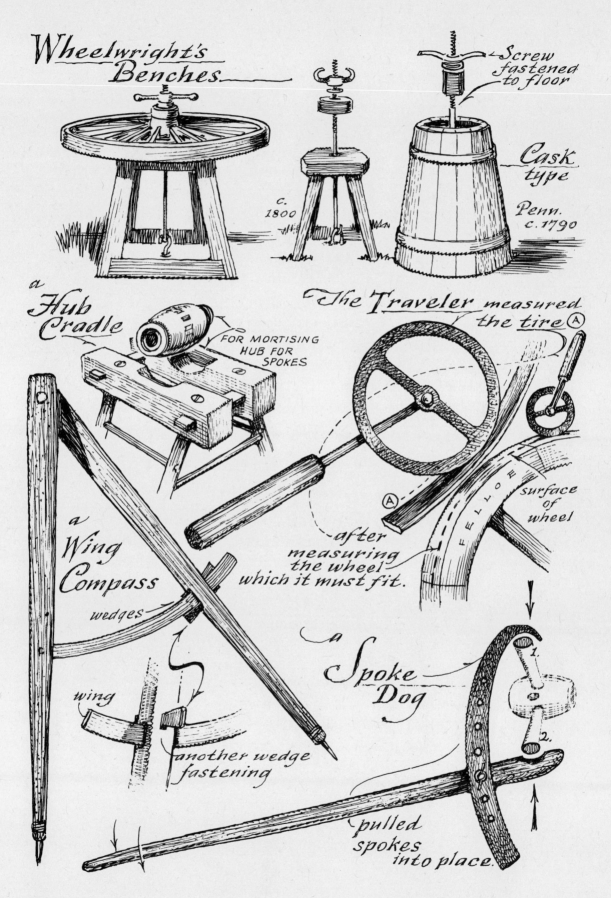

Wheelwright's Benches

c. 1800

Screw fastened to floor

Cask type

Penn. c. 1790

a **Hub Cradle**

FOR MORTISING HUB FOR SPOKES

The **Traveler** *measured the tire* Ⓐ

after measuring the wheel which it must fit.

FELLOE

surface of wheel

Ⓐ

a **Wing Compass**

wedges

wing

another wedge fastening

a **Spoke Dog**

1.

2.

pulled spokes into place.

It's all in the Way you Hit it.

Today we think a hammer is a hammer—the same thing that lays a roof, cracks a nut! But the early craftsman (like a good golfer) knew that *how* you hit and *what you hit with* could make a difference in the job being done. See, in the drawing below, how the flail separates the grain while the pestle grinds it; yet both tools hit.

The "flinting pick" did the job of making gun flints; the "bricklayer's hammer" and "axe" and "raker" did work that is still admired after two centuries. The "printing mallet" stamped designs on painted floor cloths (popular before linoleum). The "flood gate hammer" didn't smash the gate; its massive weight just moved it. The "zax" cut roofing slate and made nail holes in it. The "trunnel hammer" knocked trunnels in without smashing them. And so on. Each "hammer" hit a special kind of blow to do the specialty the craftsman needed done.

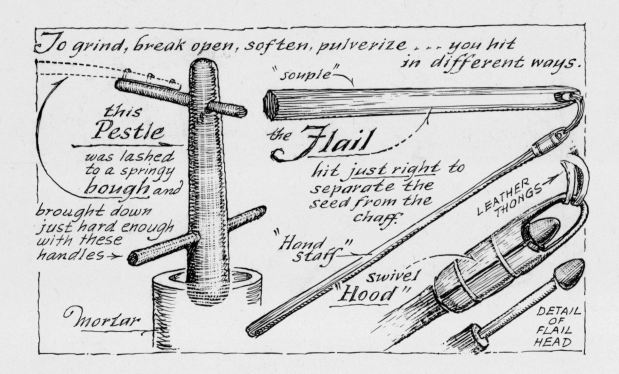

To grind, break open, soften, pulverize . . . you hit in different ways.

this Pestle was lashed to a springy bough and brought down just hard enough with these handles →

Mortar

"souple"

the Flail hit just right to separate the seed from the chaff.

"Hand staff"

swivel "Hood"

LEATHER THONGS

DETAIL OF FLAIL HEAD

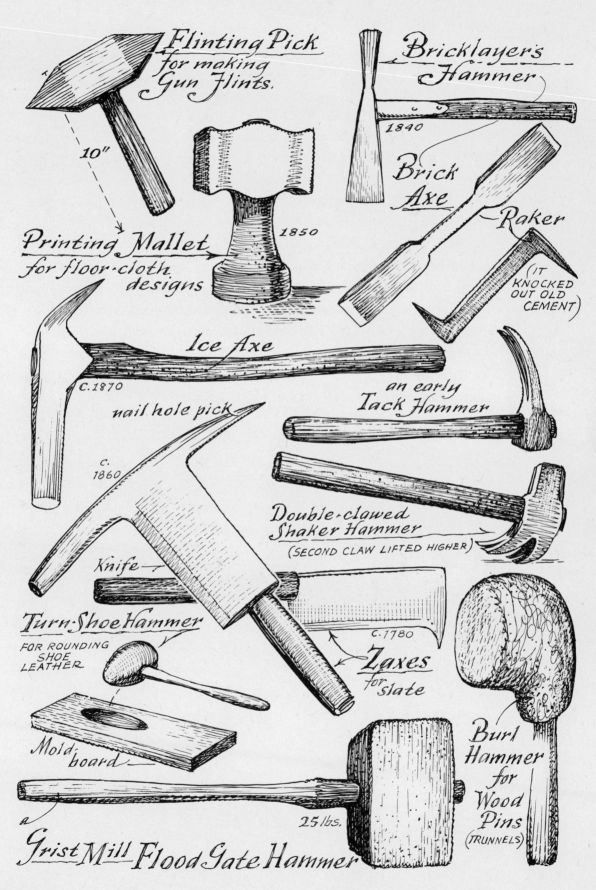

Flinting Pick for making Gun Flints.

Bricklayer's Hammer

1840

Brick Axe

Raker (IT KNOCKED OUT OLD CEMENT)

10"

Printing Mallet for floor-cloth designs

1850

Ice Axe

C. 1870

nail hole pick

an early Tack Hammer

C. 1860

Double-clawed Shaker Hammer (SECOND CLAW LIFTED HIGHER)

Knife

Turn-Shoe Hammer
FOR ROUNDING SHOE LEATHER

C. 1780

Zaxes for slate

Burl Hammer for Wood Pins (TRUNNELS)

Mold board

a

25 lbs.

Grist Mill Flood Gate Hammer

99

Hay Implements

Among the more plentiful old barn relics is the hay knife. Wide, heavy and with the blade on the outer edge, most people wonder how hay could be reaped with it. It didn't reap—it cut out portions of hay from the haystack. The hay-spade and hay-saw did the same thing. The hay-spade knife, however, doubled as pumpkin cutter in the days when pumpkins were animal food. Pumpkin stalks tended to choke animals, so pumpkins were cut from the top and the stalks destroyed.

The slender, sharp reaping hook became an American design of rare beauty by the late 1700's. But during the late 1800's the art of cutting gave way to the art of slashing, and a sickle is a better slasher. The earliest corn knife was machetelike, but the sicklelike corn knife appeared in the early 1800's.

The sickle reaped with the aid of a grass crook (hay crook), which was also used for pulling loose hay from the stack.

Although such serrations are usually worn away in ancient tools, the early sickles were usually serrated; this sets them apart from the slender reaping hook.

This Connecticut Hay Knife c. 1850 worked like a saw.

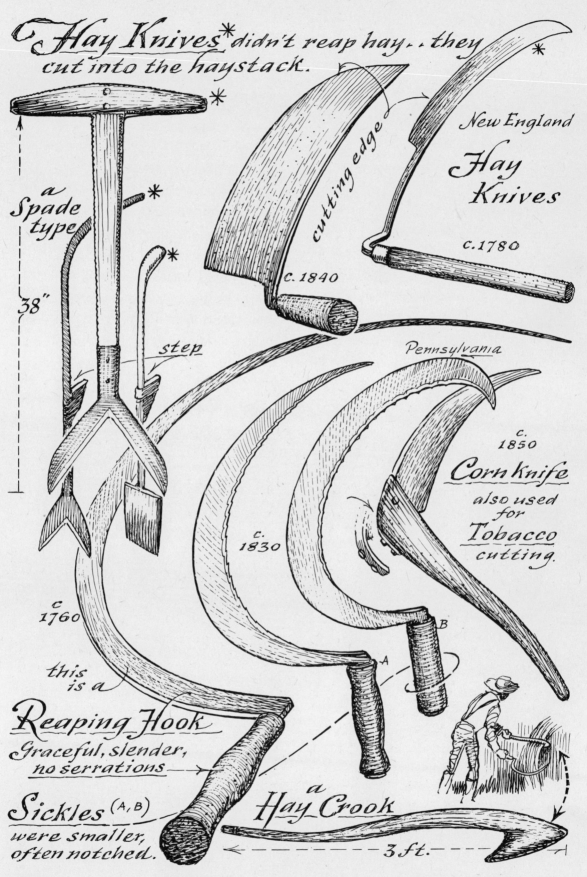

Hay Knives didn't reap hay.. they cut into the haystack.

a Spade type

38"

step

cutting edge

New England Hay Knives
c. 1780

c. 1840

Pennsylvania

c. 1850

Corn Knife
also used for *Tobacco* cutting.

c. 1830

c. 1760

B

A

this is a

Reaping Hook
Graceful, slender, no serrations

Sickles (A, B)
were smaller, often notched.

a Hay Crook

← ——— 3 ft. ——— →

Knives and Grass

The first American grass blades were from England and matched to naturally bent "snaths" (handles) without "nibs" (hand grips). Our early scythes and cradle scythes were things of rare grace. Even those of the 1800's that were factory-made retained the lines that made them different from the cruder European and English implements. The snath was usually made of willow, shaped in hot oil; the nibs and fingers of hickory; the sned of ash. Wire rods were added in the late 1800's.

The scythes and forks of America before the late 1800's will someday be prized as pieces of art, but as of now they are so large or cumbersome that few choose to collect them. You are almost never likely to see an ancient wooden rake or scythe broken, although those made during the last seventy-five years or so have an average life of about five to ten years.

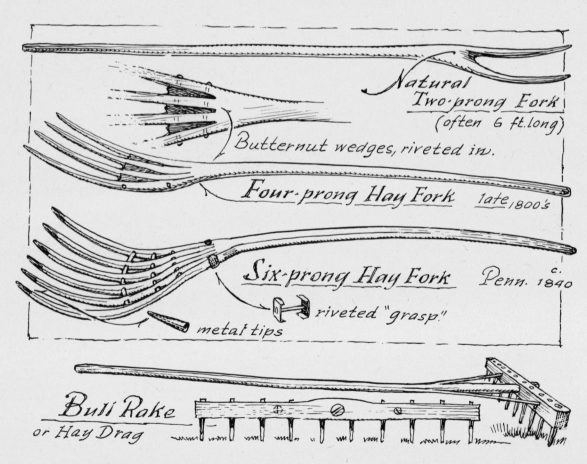

Natural Two-prong Fork (often 6 ft. long)

Butternut wedges, riveted in.

Four-prong Hay Fork late 1800's

Six-prong Hay Fork Penn. c. 1840

riveted "grasp."

metal tips

Bull Rake or Hay Drag

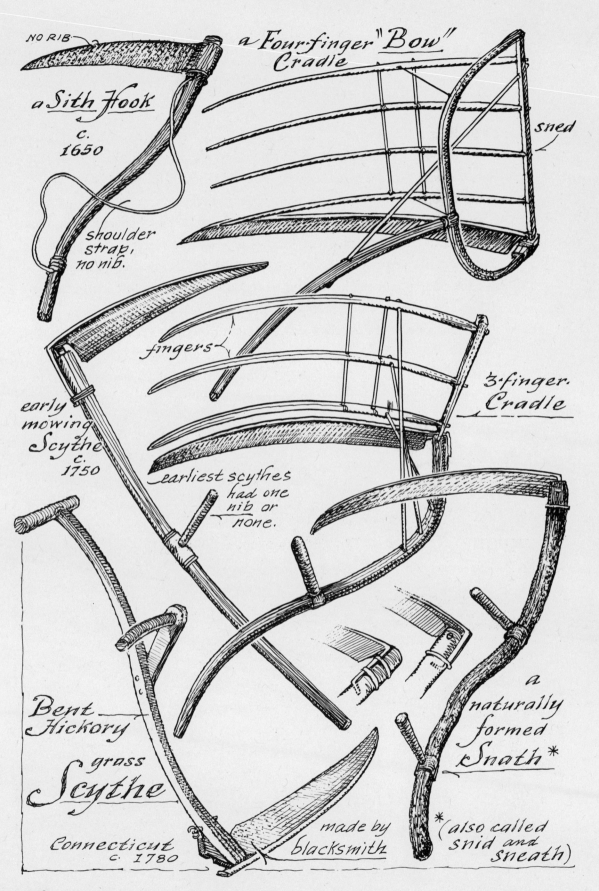

NO RIB.

a *Sith Hook*
c. 1650

a *Four-finger "Bow" Cradle*

sned

shoulder strap, no nib.

fingers

3-finger. Cradle

early mowing *Scythe* c. 1750

earliest scythes had one nib or none.

Bent Hickory gross Scythe

a naturally formed *Snath**

made by blacksmith

Connecticut c. 1780

(also called snid and sneath)

Found in the Barn

Oddities now, common items a century ago, here are a few things that were found in old barns and brought to me for identification. A tiny yoke for a goose, a cheesemaker's curd cutter and stirrer, a big winnowing scoop one used to throw flailed grain into the air to let the wind blow away the chaff—these are things that bring the past back vividly. Most old barns have eel spears tucked away near the rafters, although there may not be a river or lake for miles around. Yet a century ago men prized their swamp and wetlands, and stored up water in millponds for water-power instead of bulldozing over the wet places as we do now.

The American countryside was very different a century or two ago!

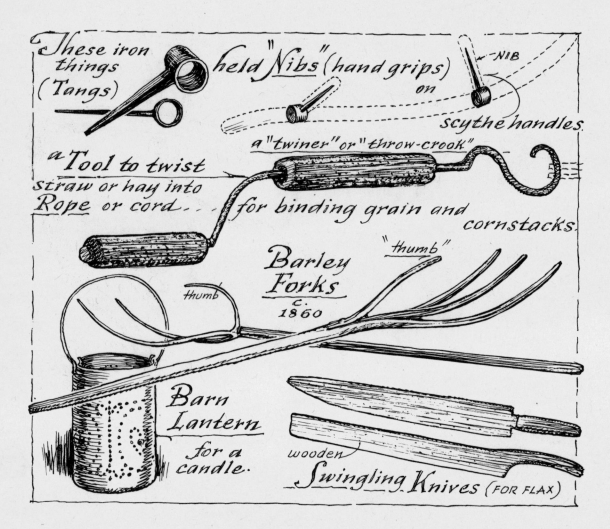

These iron things (Tangs) held "Nibs" (hand grips) on scythe handles. — NIB

a "twiner" or "throw-crook"

a Tool to twist straw or hay into Rope or cord... for binding grain and cornstacks.

Barley Forks c. 1860

"thumb"

thumb

Barn Lantern for a candle.

wooden

Swingling Knives (FOR FLAX)

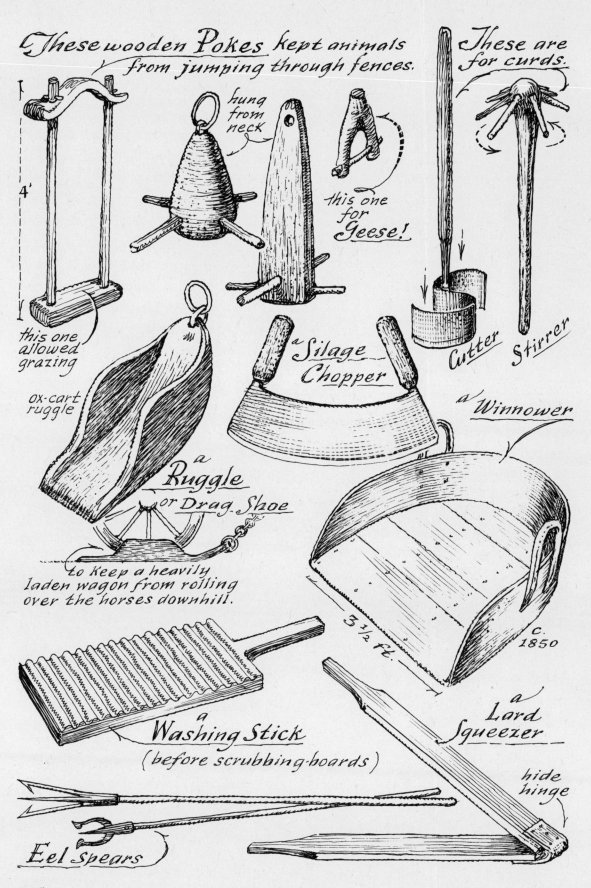

These wooden Pokes kept animals from jumping through fences.

These are for curds.

hung from neck

this one for Geese!

4'

this one allowed grazing

Cutter

Stirrer

ox-cart ruggle

a Silage Chopper

a Winnower

a Ruggle or Drag Shoe

to keep a heavily laden wagon from rolling over the horses downhill.

3½ ft.

c. 1850

a Washing Stick

(before scrubbing-boards)

a Lard Squeezer

hide hinge

Eel Spears

Index

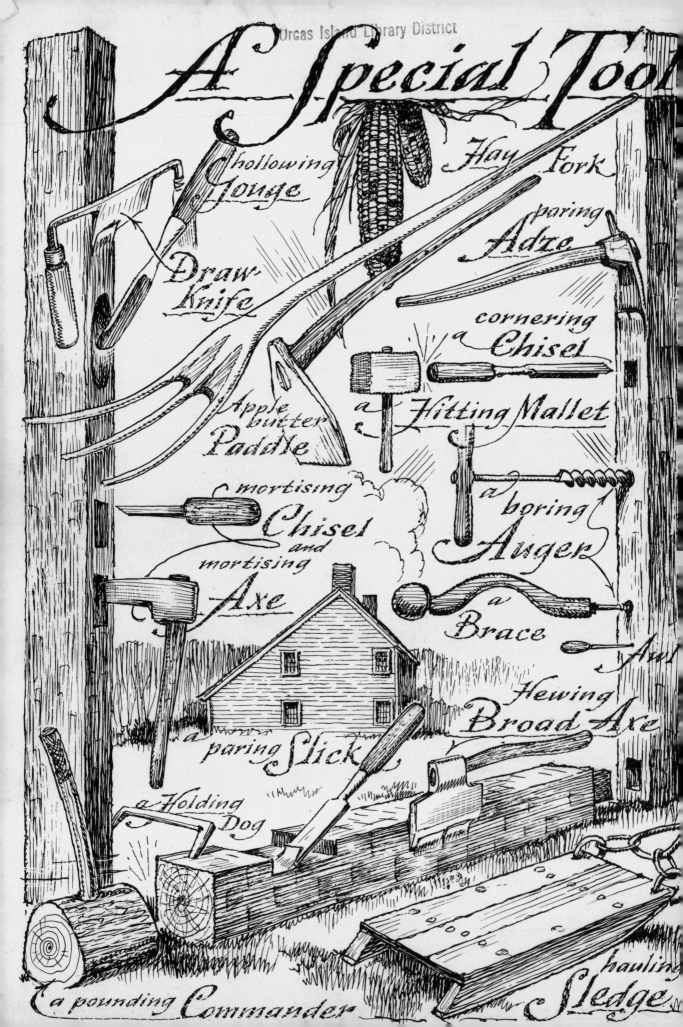